D0114007

THE GREAT LITTLE MADISON

Jean Fritz

illustrated with prints and engravings

The Putnam & Grosset Group

*With gratitude for the careful
reading that Dr. Ralph Ketcham
gave the manuscript.*

Text copyright © 1989 by Jean Fritz
All rights reserved. This book, or parts thereof, may
not be reproduced in any form without permission in
writing from the publisher. A PaperStar Book, published
in 1998 by The Putnam & Grosset Group, 200 Madison
Avenue, New York, NY 10016. PaperStar is a
registered trademark of The Putnam Berkley Group, Inc.
The PaperStar logo is a trademark of The Putnam Berkley
Group, Inc. Originally published in 1989 by G. P. Putnam's Sons.
Published simultaneously in Canada
Printed in the United States of America
Book design by Christy Hale
Library of Congress Cataloging-in-Publication Data
Fritz, Jean. The great little Madison / Jean Fritz.
p.   cm.   Bibliography: p. Summary: Traces the life and
contributions of the sickly child with the small voice who grew up
to become the fourth president of the United States.
1. Madison, James, 1751-1836—Juvenile literature.
2. Presidents—United States—Biography—Juvenile literature.
[1. Madison James, 1751-1836. 2. Presidents.] I. Title.
E342.F75 1989 973.5´1´0924—dc19 [B] [92] 88-31584 CIP AC
ISBN 0-698-11621-6

1 3 5 7 9 10 8 6 4 2

To Gina Maccoby

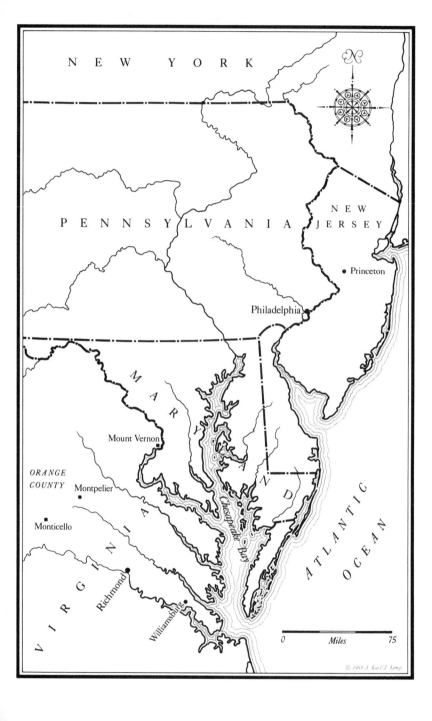

One

J ames Madison was a small, pale, sickly boy with a weak voice. If he tried to shout, the shout shriveled up in his throat, but of course he was still young. His voice might grow as he did. Or he might never need a big voice.

So far he got along fine on his father's Virginia plantation where nothing much changed but the weather and the seasons and the coming of babies. There would be twelve babies in the Madison family before they quit coming. (Five died young.) James, or Jemmy, as his father called him, was the oldest and if he was like his father and his grandfather before him, he'd spend his life on this land, bounded in the west by the lovely blue line of mountains that seemed to mark the end of the world. In 1760 when nine-year-old James helped his father move the furniture from their old house to the new brick one that looked square at the mountains, James understood that this house and the 5000 acres that went with it would one day belong to him. James loved this place. Particularly the trees. The grove of walnuts where he played with his brothers and sisters and the black children who belonged to the plantation. The two tulip trees that were so much alike, they were called "The Twins." And his favorite—the redbuds that turned themselves into pink froth every springtime.

Still, he knew there was more to the world than his father's 5000 acres, more than was contained in his own Orange County or in Virginia itself. At nine he was reading, and although he had always asked questions of his own (Where do the redbirds fly in winter?), he was discovering in his father's library questions he would never have thought of asking. His father had eighty-five books and by the time he was eleven, James had read them all. They had titles like *The Duty of Man, The Employment of the Microscope.* There was one on cold bathing; one on children's diseases. He may have been especially interested in the diseases for he was sick a great deal. All his life he suffered from fever, bilious attacks (liver upsets), and from occasional seizures in which for a few moments he would stiffen and lose control of his mind. A doctor diagnosed this as a form of epilepsy caused by nerves, but James simply called it a "falling sickness." In any case, sickness didn't often keep him from reading. Nothing ever would.

But here he was, eleven years old and there was not another book in the house to read. So Mr. Madison sent him off to a school in a neighboring county where he had all the books he wanted. He learned French so he could read books that were written in French and he learned Latin and Greek so he could find out what men thought hundreds of years

Madison's "universe"

ago. He studied geometry and algebra and the history of other nations, and to show just how much bigger his notion of the world had become, he drew a picture of the universe in his copybook. All the planets were there and the sun, a big round circle in the center. Then in order to give his universe a more friendly look, he gave the sun a face—eyes, nose, and a mouth that was almost ready to smile. Best of all, however, was his teacher, Mr. Robertson, who raised all kinds of questions (Were there people on those planets?) and made his pupils use logic and reason when they spoke. He couldn't make James speak any louder, but he did make sure that when he did speak, he had something to say.

James stayed at Mr. Robertson's school until he was sixteen and would like to have stayed longer, but his father called him home. A new minister (Mr. Martin) was living with them now, and he could teach James along with the oldest of his brothers and sisters. At the same time he would prepare James to enter college. The College of New Jersey (Princeton) was the place Mr. Madison and Mr. Martin picked. Most young men in Virginia attended the nearby College of William and Mary, but that wouldn't do for James. Too much drinking and partying at that school. Besides, the climate was not healthy.

In the summer of 1769 when James was eighteen years old, he set out on horseback for New Jersey, accompanied by Mr. Martin. He didn't look old enough to be going to college, although actually he was older than most. His face still had that young, unset, waiting look. And he was little. At five feet six, he was not excessively short, but because he was thin with a slight build and narrow shoulders, people were forever remarking on his littleness. His voice was still little too. Moreover, he was shy. Only when he knew a person well did he speak of what was going on inside him.

He did know Mr. Martin, so he would not have been afraid to show his excitement, particularly when they reached Philadelphia. He had known, of course, that Philadelphia was the biggest city in the country, but how could he have guessed that the bigness, the busyness, the importance of the city would give it such a throb of life? This was obviously where things were happening; this is where life was running at full tilt.

In its own way the college at Princeton was also exciting. People were asking questions that struck at the very core of life. What is government? What is man? Because James was ahead of the freshman class in his studies, he entered as a sophomore and perhaps this was the happiest year of his college life. He made close friends, devoured books as if he couldn't get enough of them, and joined in student fun—

Young Madison

putting greasy feathers on the floor where fellow students would slip on them, setting off firecrackers in newcomers' rooms, and eyeing girls through telescopes.

And for the first time James felt caught up in affairs that were affecting the whole country. Over the last five years he had been concerned, as everyone was, about Great Britain's aggravating policy of slapping down taxes on the colonies. But at Princeton he felt that he was reacting as part of an aroused body, as if he and his friends *were* the colonies. They approved of the fact that American merchants in protest over taxation had stopped buying goods from England, but in 1770 when the merchants of New York wrote to the merchants of Pennsylvania, suggesting that they break this

College at Princeton

agreement, the students were enraged. James Madison was one of many who marched onto the campus, cheering as a copy of that New York letter was thrown into a bonfire. The college bells tolled throughout the demonstration as if they were grieving for the liberty of the country. Flushed with patriotism, James cheered as loud as he could. His cheer may not have amounted to much, but his whole heart was in it.

James loved his Princeton years, so it is surprising that he wanted to finish them so quickly. He and a friend, Joe Ross, applied for and received permission to take their last two years in one year. What was the hurry? Perhaps James was trying to cut down expenses for his father. Perhaps he was worrying about his future. After all, he was at college to prepare himself for something, but what? He could not bear the idea of simply settling down on his father's plantation, which managed quite well without him. He wished he could find a life for himself that had nothing to do with slaves. He hated slavery, but the South was so deep into it, he didn't see how it could get out. The only way he could escape was to find a career of his own. He listened to his friends talk of their plans for the future. Most were choosing to be preachers or lawyers, but how could James be either? With his weak voice, how could he stand up in a pulpit and deliver a thundering sermon about the will of God? How could he speak out in a courtroom and convince a jury that he was right? (Besides, he didn't want to.) Perhaps he worked so hard because he needed to prove himself. Or forget himself. Perhaps without realizing it, he was simply trying to overcome his littleness.

It was a terrible schedule that he and Joe Ross set themselves. For the most part James tried to get by with no more than five hours of sleep a night. He must have felt his body breaking under the strain but he didn't give up. He finished his work in time to get his degree but he wasn't at the graduation ceremony with his ten classmates. One of his collegemates, Aaron Burr, received a prize for spelling; all in his class gave speeches, but James was too sick to attend. Still, sick or well, would James have tried to deliver a speech in that little voice of his?

He was so sick, he couldn't make the trip home when college was over so he stayed on, studying Hebrew and theology under the guidance of the college president. Perhaps his father suspected that James was simply delaying his homecoming; in any case, in April, 1772, he sent for him. Come home and teach the younger children, he wrote.

James went. It was a hard, tiring, week-long ride from Philadelphia, and when he finally arrived home, he must have been suddenly overwhelmed by what lay ahead. It was as if he'd been trapped into the slow motion of the seasons. Almost as if he'd never gone to college, never been excited by books. As everyone could see, James was not suffering from his usual sickness; he was going through a physical and emotional breakdown. Not even the flowering redbud trees could raise his spirits. He taught the children, but that only took a few hours a day, and he read. But to what purpose? He tried studying law but found it, like everything else, boring. And then one day a letter came from a college friend with the news that Joe Ross had died.

Now he had grief to add to his depression and he must have asked himself if Joe had been suffering in the way he had. Perhaps this was the inevitable result of two years of grinding overwork. In any case, James became obsessed with the idea that he, too, would die young.

James's father sent him to Warm Springs, a health resort whose mineral waters were supposed to cure all kinds of illness. James drank gallons of water, but still he came home, no better. His doctor advised more exercise. Go out and ride horseback, he said, and actually this did seem to help. In the end, however, it was not anything that happened on the plantation but what was happening in the country itself that brought James back to life.

"I do not meddle in Politicks," he wrote once to a college friend, but when at Christmas, 1773, this friend wrote him about Boston's dumping British tea into Boston harbor rather than paying tax on it, he was as excited as if he'd done the dumping himself. The following year he was strong enough to take his brother William to Princeton, where he was entering school. Of course, he had to go through Philadelphia, and his pulse quickened as it always did in the center of so much life. This time the city was at a pitch of excitement for the Continental Congress was meeting here with delegates from all thirteen colonies, waving questions like flags, challenging the future. How much longer would America put up with Great Britain? Should the country be preparing for war? James Madison came away moved by the *oneness* of America. Separate colonies they might be, but here they were, acting in union, striving for the right to govern themselves. *Our* right, he would have said, for James counted himself in the struggle.

At about this same time (September 1774) James bought two hundred acres of his father's farm for himself. He needed to own land in his own right if he wanted to vote or hold office. In December he and his father were both elected to the Orange County Committee of Safety, whose job was to see that the county was prepared to fight and to make sure that everyone in the county was loyal to America. Anyone who still stuck up for England was called a Tory and would be punished.

James entered enthusiastically into the work of the committee. He knew he could never be a regular soldier because of his "falling sickness," but he did become a member of the local militia. He was commissioned a colonel, and although on his first day of drill he fainted on the parade ground, this did not discourage him. In letters to his friends he was soon bragging about his marksmanship. If he had to, he said, he could hit a man full in the face at the distance of one hundred yards. As for Tories or suspected Tories, no penalty was too severe for them. One man who showed disrespect for a committee member was tarred and feathered, and according to James, this was no more than he deserved. If other states didn't know what to do with their traitors, he said, just send them down to Orange County. His committee would take care of them.

Shooting and tar and feathering may have given James an outlet for his passion for independence, but of course what James was best at (and had always been best at) was reasoning. In May 1776, when it was becoming clear that King George III was not going to back down, James Madison was elected to represent Orange County at a state convention in Williamsburg. On May 15 the convention voted unanimously (James along with everyone else) to instruct the Virginia delegates at the Continental Congress in Philadelphia to propose a Declaration of Independence. Six weeks later independence was declared. James Madison was only twenty-five years old and he might have thought that at last he had found his career, but he probably gave his own future little thought. It was only the country that concerned him. America had a chance now to become an independent nation, and it had better turn out to be a good one.

Two

Americans had actually been at war a little more than a year when the Declaration of Independence was signed. The questions now were: Could they win the war? And how were they to govern themselves in the meantime? In Williamsburg the Virginia Convention set to work to draw up a state constitution. James Madison was put on a committee to consider exactly what rights every citizen in Virginia had that could not be taken away by the government or anyone else. Inalienable rights, they were called. At informal gatherings outside the convention, James made friends and felt free to say what he pleased. But never once in the convention itself did he speak out. Still, one of his new friends, Edmund Randolph, reported that James was fantastic at whispering. Indeed, Edmund tried to sit next to him at meetings because James always had interesting comments to whisper in his ear.

James was not only quiet but apparently tried to be inconspicuous as well. He often wore black with buckles at the knees of his breeches and black silk stockings. (Later he would wear nothing but black.) Following the fashion of his time, he powdered his hair (dark brown under the powder) and wore it pulled back and tied behind. On his head he wore a black hat with a cone-shaped crown that was high but didn't seem to make him look taller. One delegate wrote: "Madison was probably the only small man at the convention."

And of course he was conscious of his small voice. Even if he dared speak out, how would his voice carry before so many men? Just looking at the famous orator Patrick Henry must have made him uneasy. All Mr. Henry had to do was

Patrick Henry

open his mouth and that mighty voice of his would fill the room and set it quivering. When he wasn't talking, Mr. Henry looked down his long nose at the other delegates as if they were common dirt. Even so, sometimes it was hard for James to keep quiet. He had strong ideas about the questions they were discussing. Religion, in particular.

Nothing made James angrier than to see men punished for their religious views. And they often were. Baptists and Presbyterians were the ones most frequently picked on because they were not members of the church of England or established church. Only recently five or six people in his own part of Virginia had been thrown in jail because of religious opinions that they had expressed. Furious, James wrote to a college friend: "I have squabbled and scolded abused and ridiculed so long about it . . . I am without common patience." He would never have patience when it came to religious freedom, which was certainly one of the inalienable rights. He was against anyone "making laws for the human mind," and again and again throughout his life he would fight to see that the state had no hold over a person's religious beliefs or expression.

Now at the Virginia convention James found himself objecting to the way the resolution on religion was worded. It stated that all men should enjoy the fullest toleration in the exercise of religion. Toleration! That wasn't enough for James. He couldn't abide such weak wording, so he wrote out his proposed version. "All men are equally entitled to enjoy the free *exercise* of religion." His revision was approved.

When James went home in December after the session in Williamsburg had adjourned, he had made up his mind that in the spring he would run for election to the Virginia House of Delegates, the new legislative body of the colony. Of course where he'd really like to be was in Philadelphia where the Continental Congress was working out problems for the whole country. From what he had heard, he thought they could use some help. James read every newspaper he could lay his hands on. He rejoiced over General Washington's victory at Trenton and again at Princeton. He helped his father round up supplies for the army. And he read. He wanted to understand how governments worked, how some had fallen in the past, some succeeded. The whole question, he decided, turned on where the power lay. In Virginia, he suspected, the people had already made mistakes in their new constitution. So afraid of tyranny, they had given the governor too little power and the House of Delegates too much. In any case, he would soon have the chance to study all this at first hand. He more or less took for granted that he would win the election. After all, he was well known in the county and people seemed to be impressed by his book learning. Besides, how could he stand on the sidelines of America? He *had* to win.

But he didn't. His opponent, an older man, followed the old Virginia custom of setting out a barrel of whisky in front of the courthouse and treating the voters as they came to the polls. James thought this was old-fashioned nonsense. He expected people to vote with their heads, with or without whisky, so he provided no drinks on election day. Perhaps the voters had originally intended to vote for James Madison, but if so, they changed their minds. He was either stingy or proud, they decided, and he ought to take up preaching instead of politics.

James brooded, but not for long. In the fall the House of Delegates voted for James to fill a vacancy in the eight-man Council of State (which, with the governor, made up the executive branch of the government). James served for two years, and as people came to know him, they discovered his talents. In behind-the-scenes political discussions James was strong and persuasive and, as Patrick Henry, who was governor, soon found out, James wrote easily and clearly. Patrick Henry might be able to send his voice to the rafters, but he disliked descending to a desk and dealing with pen and paper. So he gave James the job of writing up state papers. But the most important thing that happened to James was that he made friends with Thomas Jefferson.

The two men had known each other for some time, but they were thrown more closely together when in June 1779 Jefferson was elected governor to succeed Patrick Henry. As a member of the governor's council, Madison discovered not only how well he and Jefferson worked together but how much they had in common. Tall, red-headed, thirty-six-year-old Jefferson and small, twenty-eight-year-old Madison shared the same vision of a strong, united republican government. They both liked the same things: reading and collecting books, planting trees, experimenting with science, talking about history. And they agreed on what they didn't like: Great Britain, slavery, the lopsided Virginia constitution, and Patrick Henry. Neither man could stand Patrick Henry. "What shall we do with him?" James asked once when Patrick was being obstructive in his usual eloquent way. "What we have to do, I think," Jefferson replied, "is devoutly pray for his death."

It was a lifelong friendship that Madison and Jefferson established, although they would often have to depend on letters for news of each other. In December 1779 they were separated when James was elected a delegate to the Continental Congress in Philadelphia. James went home first and planned to go on from there, but like everyone else in Virginia (and throughout the country) he became snowbound. It

Thomas Jefferson

was the coldest winter of the war. In Morristown, New Jersey, where the army was quartered, the soldiers were running out of food. "The troops, both officers and men," George Washington wrote, "have been almost perishing for want." Of course had they stopped to think, there were things that everyone could be thankful for. Philadelphia, which had been occupied by the British, was back in American hands and had been for more than a year. The French were fighting on America's side. But in Morristown the soldiers' stomachs were too empty for them to think of anything but their next meal. And the British army. It had holed up in nearby New York.

James Madison arrived in Philadelphia on March 18, 1780, soon after his twenty-ninth birthday. As was fitting for a delegate to the Congress, he brought a servant with him (his slave Billey) and settled down in a boardinghouse, ready for life in Philadelphia. Jefferson, who had been a delegate to the Continental Congress, would have told him about the city's social life, but still James may have been surprised at just how lively it was. Indeed the way Philadelphians entertained, one would have hardly known that the country was at war. Women spent entire afternoons dressing their hair into such towering beehives that when they went out in the evening, they had to scrunch down in their carriages to keep their hairdos from scraping the roofs. (Peggy Shippen, the future wife of Benedict Arnold, had to hang her head out of the carriage window.) Of course these stylish hostesses were curious about the young, newly arrived bachelor from Virginia, but one, who invited him to a party, was not impressed. He was a "gloomy, stiff creature," she said, "with nothing engaging or even bearable about his manners."

At first Madison didn't open his mouth in Congress. He served on committees, worked behind the scenes as he had in Virginia, but at the regular meetings he simply listened. And he was sickened by what he heard. Although all wanted to win the war, they could not agree on practical measures for governing. They had a hard time even sending the army all it needed to survive. It would be another year before Congress would ratify the Articles of Confederation, the nearest thing the country had to a constitution or "law of the land."

Not that this would help Madison. In Madison's opinion the Articles were "imbecilic." "A firm league of friendship"—that's what the Articles claimed to be, but where was the friendship among states that showed more interest in maintaining their own rights than in sacrificing for the common good? The Articles gave Congress no power to force the states to do anything for the central government, and in consequence they didn't do much of anything.

James wrote in disgust to Jefferson that nothing was going as it should. Congress needed more power; it needed better statesmen; it needed permanent solutions, not flimsy patchwork measures; and it certainly needed money. James might be a Virginian, but first and foremost he was and always would be an American pushing for a genuine union of the states.

James held his tongue for six months and then, whether he could be heard or not, he spoke out. His voice was as feeble as it had always been and, indeed, he didn't present much of a figure—this small man with a habit of rocking back and forth on his feet as he warmed to his subject. The delegates might smile. "No bigger than a half a piece of soap," one observed. They might strain to hear him, but as time went on, they had to agree that James Madison had sound judgment.

And as time went on, so did the war. When the British Army moved out of New York in the spring, it moved south, and although there were spurts of good news now and then from the American forces, most of the news was bad. The fall of Charleston, South Carolina, in May 1780—that was the worst. Then a month later the British decided they would pounce on members of the Virginia House of Delegates, which was holding an emergency meeting in Charlottesville, Virginia. From there, they would climb the hill to

Monticello, Jefferson's home. Luckily, the delegates were warned in time and most (thirty-three including Patrick Henry) managed to escape. Seven delegates either didn't take the warning seriously or were natural slowpokes; in any case, they were captured. As for Thomas Jefferson, though he sent his family away at the first hint of trouble, he stayed until he had looked through his telescope and had actually seen the redcoats on the streets of Charlottesville. Then he too made his getaway.

All this was taking place not more than thirty miles from James Madison's own home in Orange. (Since all the great homes in Virginia had names, the Madisons called theirs Montpelier now.) Had he known what was happening at the time, James would have been enraged. Already he had heard enough stories of the British Army's cruelty to civilians in Virginia that his hatred of England became so bitter, it stayed with him for life. But news traveled slowly, and by the time it reached Philadelphia, James had heard that Montpelier and his friend Thomas Jefferson were safe, and he had himself escaped from a near accident. But not from the British. A bolt of lightning had struck his boarding house; entering the chimney and conducted by a bell ring, it ran through several rooms. Luckily no one was hurt, but why hadn't they paid attention to Dr. Franklin? they asked themselves. Why hadn't they put up one of his electric rods?

In the fall, the attention of the country was suddenly centered on Yorktown, a small Virginia settlement on Chesapeake Bay. The Americans had managed to maneuver the British under the command of General Cornwallis into a corner where if all went well, the British might be defeated. It might even be a final defeat—that is, if American reinforcements arrived in time to keep the British from escaping by land, and if the French fleet, now in the West Indies, arrived in time to keep the British from escaping by sea. In war, seldom do all "ifs" work out right, yet the people hoped and feared.

In September reinforcements left Philadelphia for Virginia. James Madison stood in front of the State House with General Washington and other delegates of Congress as three thousand Continental troops in all kinds of makeshift uniforms paraded past. Two French divisions followed, smartly dressed, marching with precision. When they reached the State House, they dropped the points of their swords and dipped their colors. In return the delegates took off their hats. It was a solemn send-off.

Six weeks of suspense lay ahead, charged with rumors, both good and bad. In the end, however, all the ifs did fall in place, and on October 19 General Cornwallis surrendered. When the news reached Philadelphia, all the members of Congress walked together to the nearby Dutch Lutheran church to give thanks. That night would have been a perfect time to set off firecrackers, and Americans did love an excuse to make a fireworks display, but the weather was too dry. There would have been danger of fire, so instead the people of Philadelphia set lighted candles in every window in the city. James Madison said he had never been happier.

At last people were beginning to understand James. Yes, he was stiff and awkward, but only when strangers were present. Among those he knew, he was, as one friend observed, "charming." Relaxed after a meal with friends, Madison was frank and lively in his conversation, delighting in telling little jokes on himself. Once in Williamsburg, he said, he left his hat on a window ledge and it was stolen. As everyone knew, no gentleman would appear outdoors with his head uncovered, but try as he might, James could not find another hat. For two days he had to stay away from the

Kitty Floyd

Governor's Palace where the Council was meeting. Finally a Frenchman who sold snuff agreed to sell him something he had. At this point Madison would start laughing, for it was such a queer-looking affair, that hat—huge, wide-brimmed, with a crown no bigger than a pimple poking up from a field of black. No one who heard the story ever forgot the picture of that enormous hat bouncing down the street to the Governor's Palace with little Mr. Madison under it.

James felt particularly at home with the group of people who lodged in the same house as he did. They liked to tease James about being such a confirmed bachelor, but in the spring of 1783 they decided that perhaps he wasn't so confirmed after all. James was thirty-two years old now, and he was obviously smitten by pretty sixteen-year-old Kitty Floyd, daughter of a New York delegate living in the same house. In the evening when the boarders (including a nineteen-year-old medical student) gathered in the parlor to hear Kitty Floyd play the harp, James (and the medical student) were clearly less interested in the music than in Miss Floyd. The fact that James was so much older than Kitty didn't discourage him. Actually it made him bolder. So he began to court her, then proposed to her, then asked her father for her hand. Since neither Kitty nor her father were against the idea, James and Kitty began planning a November wedding. Joyfully he wrote Jefferson the news in a code they had developed between them to insure secrecy. It was a complicated code, like a dictionary with words arranged alphabetically and numbers beside them that would replace words in their correspondence. Since the vocabulary was related largely to politics and business, it was a little difficult for James to talk about love. In code he said that he had "ascertained her sentiments" and the event would take place in the fall.

At the end of April Kitty and her family went home for the summer, and though he hated the separation, James tried to be patient. He couldn't have imagined that he'd be called on for more than patience, but in July Kitty wrote that she had changed her mind. She felt "indifferent" to him now and had decided to marry that nineteen-year-old medical student. She sealed the letter not with sealing wax but with a piece of rye dough. Maybe this was what was handy, but many have interpreted the rye dough as a deliberate insult.

James wrote to Jefferson and Jefferson, whose wife had died the previous year, sent his sympathy. What James had to do, Jefferson said, was to keep busy. This was the only way to get over such grief.

Well, there would be plenty for James to do. Two months later, in September, the peace treaty with Great Britain was signed and the independence of the United States was formally recognized. And now what? James asked. George Washington described the country as limping along under the Articles of Confederation, "moving upon crutches and tottering at every step." How could the country survive like this?

Key to code Jefferson and Madison used

Three

J ames had only two more months to serve before his term in the Continental Congress was over and he wanted to do what he could in the time that was left. If only the question of taxation could be resolved! As always, Americans balked at being taxed and the states balked at being required (or requested) to pay the central government a definite sum, even though the government had run up huge debts in the war, even though the government couldn't pay the soldiers all that was owed them. James had tried to add an amendment to the Articles of Confederation to take care of the taxation problem, but one Virginia delegate said he'd crawl to Richmond on his hands and knees before he'd let that go through.

For Jefferson and Madison, of course, there was always the problem of slavery, but they agreed that there was nothing that could be done at the moment. Maybe when the country became more stable, but not now. James knew, however, that it would be cruel to take his own slave Billey back to Montpelier when he went. In his four years in Philadelphia, Billey had led such a different life, he'd never adapt to the plantation again. Sometime ago James had sold him to a friend as an indentured servant, which, according to Pennsylvania law, meant that he would be set free after seven years. Meanwhile, as long as James was in Philadelphia, Billey would stay on as his valet and James would pay for him out of the little money he had. Virginia had not paid James one cent of salary during his entire time in Philadelphia. He had depended on money from home and from a patriotic Philadelphian, Haym Salomon, who was generous to other delegates as well.

One of the last things Madison did was to take part in a debate about a permanent capital for the country. Madison, as well as the other Virginians, had his heart set on a site on the Potomac River, and since New Englanders had always hated Philadelphia, he thought the Southerners had a chance to win this vote. In the end, however, six states voted for Trenton, New Jersey. Since only one more vote was needed for Trenton, the Southerners quickly proposed a compromise. Why not let the capital take turns—six months at Trenton, six months at Annapolis? The delegates were sick of arguing, so they agreed, but Madison knew that this makeshift agreement couldn't last. Sometime the Potomac would have another chance.

It had been almost four years since Madison had been back to Montpelier and of course he found changes. His youngest sister, Fanny, who was just eight when he'd left, was twelve now, almost a young lady. All three brothers were married and his sister Nelly was about to be married.

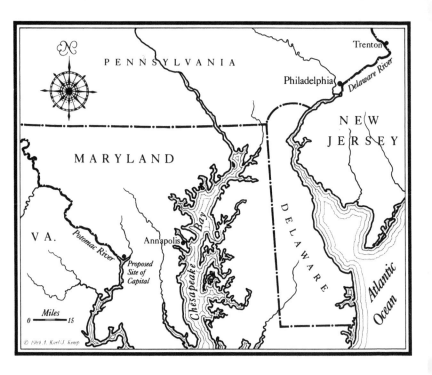

But what about James himself? The family must have joked about his staying single for so long. Couldn't he find any girls in Philadelphia? Or did he want one from the South? After all, James at thirty-two was already showing signs of becoming bald. But his family could also see that James had acquired a new kind of self-assurance. And he looked healthier. His voice hadn't grown any bigger, but at least he wasn't shy about using it.

Still, he was a worrier. All winter he worried. He studied and worried. He might stop for a game of whist in the evening, but questions were always nagging at the back of his mind. How long would the country last under those confounded Articles of Confederation? People were going bankrupt all over the country. They were arguing about trade regulations between the states. If one state opened its ports free to foreign trade, what ships would go to states which imposed taxes? Might not arguments between the states lead to fighting? And might not this create such a mix-up that foreign states would step in and try to take over? Then the country would be right back where it had started. A new constitution—that's what was needed, but not many would agree to that. Some, James suspected, would be perfectly willing to turn the country into a monarchy—king and all.

It is not surprising that in the spring of 1784 James welcomed his election to the Virginia House of Delegates, where he might do something besides worry. Perhaps he could at least start a movement to rewrite the Virginia constitution, but as it turned out, no matter what James Madison wanted to do, Patrick Henry was against it. And Richmond, where the capital was located now, was not a comfortable place to live. It was overcrowded, noisy, the streets were muddy and so filled with horses that a foreign visitor said the place looked like an Arab village.

When the session let out for the summer recess, James decided to do something he'd never done before. He would take a vacation. Jefferson had recently left for France, where he would serve as the American minister, and although he talked of James visiting him, James knew he never would. He was afraid that the long sea voyage would bring on attacks of his "falling sickness." But a "ramble" through New England—that should be safe. So in August Madison mounted his horse and set off in high spirits for the north.

He never got to New England. In Baltimore he ran into the Marquis de Lafayette, the French general who had been active in the American Revolution and who was now about to go up the Hudson River to attend the signing of an Indian treaty. Lafayette was so popular with the Americans that wherever he went, he was cheered and surrounded with ad-

Marquis de Lafayette

mirers. And indeed he was such an open, friendly, and enthusiastic man, he was hard to resist, and James didn't even try. When Lafayette invited James to accompany him and his French friends, he readily accepted. Together they went up the Hudson on a barge, and although James was seasick when they ran into two hurricanes, one right after another, he experienced no return of his "falling sickness." In fact, he had never had so much fun in his life. When they left the barge in Albany and took off through the woods, camping as they went, James was put in charge of directing the route of the march. Lafayette took care of the horses. One of the Frenchmen saw to overnight arrangements and one did the cooking. (He made fantastic soup.) The trip took longer than expected, causing James to arrive back in Richmond two weeks late for the fall season. He had to pay a fine, but he didn't care. He'd had an adventure and he had an idea. Perhaps he could buy some of the land he admired so much in the rich Mohawk Valley in New York. Later he could sell it and perhaps make enough profit so he could live without depending on slaves.

But right now in Richmond all the problems that had worried James were not only waiting but getting worse. It was not until March 1785 that even the first small step was taken to settle any of the dangerous commercial differences. Virginia and Maryland decided to talk over navigation problems on the Potomac River which ran between the two states. James Madison and Edmund Randolph were among those from Virginia who were supposed to go to the meeting, but Patrick Henry forgot to tell them when it was being held. Still, the few who were there did reach certain agreements and most important, they suggested that the two states meet every year. When Madison heard this, he saw his chance. Why not have delegates from all states meet? he asked. Perhaps they could make a uniform system for commerce for the whole country. So invitations were sent to all the states to come to Annapolis on the first Monday of September, 1786. As soon as the delegates came together, Madison figured, they would surely see that the Articles of Confederation would have to be changed. And might this not lead to the writing of a new constitution?

As Madison left for Annapolis, however, he held out little hope for such a happy solution. Three states (Connecticut, New Jersey, and Delaware) had recently declared their ports free, which in effect destroyed trade in the states that required duties in their ports. Since money from these duties helped support Congress, the government of the country was left practically penniless. Madison wrote to Jefferson in France, telling him that he didn't expect much from the Annapolis meeting except some kind of commercial reform. "To speak the truth," he said, "I almost despair even of this."

He had every reason to despair. Day after day went by and delegates who were expected simply didn't show up. Massachusetts sent no one. Pennsylvania sent only one delegate and New York sent two, Alexander Hamilton and one other. Only Delaware, New Jersey, and Virginia were fully represented. Twelve men in all, not enough to decide a thing. Fortunately, those who did come to Annapolis were for the most part men who thought of the nation in broad terms as Madison did, not state-minded men like Patrick Henry. They agreed to ask Congress to call a large convention of all the states that would go beyond commercial questions. It would actually reconsider the Articles of Confederation and decide what could be done to make the government work.

Congress set the date for this new convention on May 14,

1787. Philadelphia was the place. But would enough men actually come?

Luckily, in the early part of 1787 something happened that scared Americans all over the country. At the time no one thought it was lucky, but the fact was that people were scared into taking that convention in Philadelphia seriously. Some farmers in western Massachusetts were the ones who did the scaring. They were all men (many, veterans like their leader, Daniel Shays) who were having their farms taken away from them by the courts, and in many cases they were being jailed because they couldn't pay their debts. Why, they asked, had they fought King George when their own government turned against them when they were in trouble? They tried lawful means to solve their problems—conventions, petitions, but when these didn't work, they said, let the law go to blazes! They forcibly closed down the courts. Then as a small army they marched toward the federal arsenal in Springfield, Massachusetts, threatening to take it over and supply themselves with arms. Congress was in an uproar. This was an insurrection; it was treason. But Congress was helpless. Although the country had a secretary of war, it had no army and no money to support one. In the end, Massachusetts called out its militia, gathered volunteers, and put down the rebels before they reached Springfield.

At the time of Shays's Rebellion, many people did not understand what lay behind the farmers' violence. All they could see was that law and order were breaking down and the country was headed for chaos. The convention at Philadelphia had better find a way to fix things. Make the central government stronger, some said. But not too strong, others added. Not strong enough to hurt the sovereignty of the states. But there were also those who were suspicious of any-

A brawl during Shays's Rebellion

thing the convention might do. Patrick Henry, for instance, looked down his long nose at the whole idea. He "smelt a rat," he said, and he'd have nothing to do with the goings-on in Philadelphia.

Except for Rhode Island, all the states did send delegates to the convention, but they trickled into Philadelphia all through the month of May. The New Hampshire men didn't arrive until July, and one man from Delaware didn't make it until August. James Madison was the first to arrive—eleven days early—and by May 25 when at last there were enough men to start business officially, he was ready with a plan.

He didn't want the convention wasting time, fussing with the old Articles of Confederation, trying to patch them up here and there. No. Let the Virginia delegates start right off with a plan for an entirely new form of government with a constitution that would replace the old Articles and be supreme over the states. And let Edmund Randolph be the spokesman. He was tall, handsome, imposing—a well-liked, outgoing man who inspired confidence, not the kind who was likely to come up with wild ideas. But when Randolph heard the three main resolutions, he was afraid that they did sound wild, especially the first, which stated flat out that the country could not get along under the Articles of Confederation, and the third resolution, which stated that a *national* government ought to be established that would be *supreme*. Madison agreed to tone down those resolutions into one simple one: "Resolved, That the Articles of Confederation ought to be corrected and enlarged as to accomplish common defense, security of liberty, and general welfare."

Randolph was more comfortable with this wording, even though he went right on to describe a government that would be supreme over the states, one with the power to force the states to fulfill their duties to the Union. One delegate immediately pointed out the contradiction. This was no correction of the Articles of Confederation, he said; this was a proposal for a new constitution and a national government. Well, there it was. Out in the open. And the floor didn't cave in; no delegates fainted; no one walked out. For James Madison, it must have seemed that at least the path had been laid down, however it was followed, however it was changed. It was as if his life and the country's were coming to a head at the same time, peaking together. His whole soul, all his pas-

Edmund Randolph

sion, all his will were centered in this hot room in Philadelphia where the flies buzzed and the future of the country lay in the hands of fifty-five unpredictable men.

James sat in the front of the room taking notes of what was said—not because he'd been asked to (there was a secretary), but because this was history and he was in the center of it and wanted the record to be straight. It was to be a secret record, just as the meeting itself was to be secret so the delegates would feel free to say what they pleased, change their minds as often as they wanted without the public butting in and hashing it over. Sitting right in front of James on a raised platform was the president of the convention, George Washington, whose very presence gave a sense of urgency to the meeting, just as James had known it would. He had put Washington's name down at the head of the list of Virginia delegates before he had even asked him. Only later did James persuade Washington how important his attendance would be. (It was too soon to mention that if a new government were formed people would feel safer because of course everyone knew that Washington would be elected president.)

The government began to take shape under Madison's pen as it scurried to keep up with the arguments, the resolutions, the votes. There would be three branches to the government: the executive, the judicial, and the legislative, which in turn

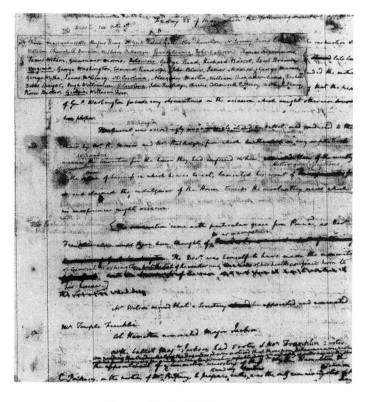

**Notes taken by Madison at the
Constitutional Convention**

would consist of two houses—the Senate and the House of Representatives. Eventually it was decided that in the Senate the states would have an equal vote; in the House the number of representatives would be determined by the population of the state. In the meantime, however, thrashing around at the bottom of every debate was the question of the division of power. Between the executive and the legislature. Between the small states and the large. Between those who wanted power to lie directly in the hands of the people and those who didn't trust the people. Madison was diligent in his note-taking, but he could not sit still when the delegates didn't seem to be grasping the importance of an issue. He knew his voice was weak but he couldn't help that. Two hundred times he spoke during the convention, and although there were often shouts of "Louder," the delegates knew they could count on him to bring reason to bear on the subject, whether they agreed with him or not.

At first the delegates allowed Mr. Randolph's so-called Virginia Plan (or Nationalist Plan) to form the centerpiece of their discussion, but there came a day in the middle of June when the small states had had enough of Virginia's big ideas. William Paterson of New Jersey, who at five feet two was by far the shortest man at this convention, said they should stick to the old Articles of Confederation. The only new powers he would give Congress would be the right to tax and the right to regulate commerce. Otherwise Congress would operate as it had in the past—a single body in which every state would have an equal vote.

No. No. No. The unspoken "no's" of the Nationalists must have reverberated in the room before Madison could gather them together to strike back at Mr. Paterson. Nothing, however, silenced the convention as much as Alexander Hamilton, who up to this time had said very little. When he

Alexander Hamilton

did take the floor now, he kept it for six unforgettable hours while the delegates sat, unbelieving, dumbfounded. What were they to think? Here was Hamilton, an aide to Washington during the war, proposing that the chief executive be chosen for *life*. Like a king. The Senate also. And state governors were to be appointed by the national government. Had the man gone mad? the delegates asked themselves. Madison undoubtedly knew how much Hamilton admired the British constitution, but to let his ideas loose at a time like this was, to say the least, foolhardy. Perhaps, however, Madison sensed there might be a method behind Hamilton's madness, and perhaps there was. In any case, on the next day the delegates, stunned by Hamilton's outburst, decided that the Virginia Plan didn't sound so bad after all. They voted, seven to three, to reject Paterson's proposal.

But there were still harrowing days ahead. There was the day for instance, when Gunning Bedford of Delaware lost his temper. "I do not, gentlemen," he shouted, "trust you."

Then there was the day that Luther Martin of Maryland couldn't stop talking. On and on he went about his idea that the only reason to have a central government was to preserve the state governments. On and on until everyone wondered if the man would ever shut up.

And there was the day that Georgia and South Carolina said they would quit the Union rather than give up the right to import slaves. After a heated debate, the convention decided that Union was more important than interfering with slavery. At least for now. They voted not to stop the slave trade before 1808. George Mason of Virginia, a violently antislavery man, predicted that heaven would punish the country for this. James Madison said that prolonging the slave trade was "dishonorable to the American character."

Finally on September 17, 1787, the Constitution was completed, ready for the delegates to sign. Some who did not approve of the Constitution had already gone home and at the last minute three delegates refused to sign. There was no Bill of Rights, they said. The people would want their inalienable rights spelled out in the Constitution. Madison explained that the people automatically retained every right not specifically handed over to the government. Still they wouldn't sign. Edmund Randolph was one of those who backed down. His reason was that he just wasn't sure; he wanted time to think it over. Madison knew Randolph well. He could change with the shift of the wind and now he simply had a case of cold feet. In the end, Madison thought, Randolph would come around.

On the whole, Madison should have been satisfied with the Constitution. The basic outline of the Virginia Plan was intact, although Madison had been defeated on some points and had been forced to compromise on others. But James Madison took no great joy in the moment; he was just too tired to take joy in anything. For one hundred days, with the exception of a few brief recesses, he had pushed himself without let-up—writing, talking by day, talking again in the evening at informal meetings, and then late at night transcribing and filling out his notes. It almost killed him, he said.

Everyone recognized how much he'd done. Indeed, during the convention he had earned a nickname. People referred to him now as "the Great Little Madison," but he would not have been impressed. No leader in American history has had less vanity or desire for praise than James Madison.

Signing of the Constitution

Four

None of the proponents of the Constitution, including James Madison, were sure how the Constitution would actually work or if it would last, but they were infuriated to think it might not even be given a chance. And indeed when the people read the Constitution, they put up such a howl, it seemed that they might refuse to have anything to do with it. Each state was to elect representatives to send to its own ratifying convention, and only when nine states had voted to ratify would the Constitution go into effect. It was particularly important that the big states ratify—Pennsylvania, New York, Massachusetts, and Virginia, but they were the ones which were raising such a clamor.

The central government would have too much power, they

cried. The states would be lost. Before they knew it, they'd have a king. And where was a Bill of Rights? The complaints piled up and it was clear that they had to be met head-on and quickly. After all, the people had had no chance to catch up to the thinking of the delegates. They had to be educated.

So three men—Madison, Hamilton, and John Jay (known best for his diplomatic services abroad)—joined in a monumental effort to explain the Constitution to the public, and to show how impossible it was to continue under the old Articles. As for the Bill of Rights, that was no problem, they pointed out. Such a bill could be added later to the Constitution as amendments. Eighty-five essays appeared in print—fifty-one by Hamilton, twenty-nine by Madison, five by Jay. All (signed simply "Publius") were published first as letters in a New York newspaper, but eventually they were bound together as a book, *The Federalist Papers,* which is still prized today as one of our country's masterpieces. Even the name was a clever stroke. By identifying themselves as Federalists, the authors forced the opposition to take on the name "Anti-Federalist," which they resented. *They* were the true Federalists, the "Antis" insisted; those who supported the Constitution should be called "Nationalists." But like it or not, "Antis" they were, and they remained a strong negative force.

When James Madison embarked on this writing project, he was still worn out from his work at the convention. "He had an air of fatigue," one observer noted. And no wonder. He worked under great pressure, as the letters were appearing daily. He was also carrying on a wide correspondence with friends all over the country to encourage them in the struggle. In particular he wrote to Edmund Randolph. He worded his letters carefully because he knew Randolph would only change his mind about the Constitution if he thought it was entirely his own idea. (And he did—fortunately in time to support it publicly.)

On March 24, 1788, Virginia was to elect representatives to its ratifying convention. Of course Madison expected to take part in the convention. How could he take a chance that Virginia might blunder? He went home as soon as he could, but he didn't arrive until March 23, and then he was told that the county was running strong against the Constitution. He might not be elected if he didn't give a campaign speech. He hated the idea. It was too much like tooting his own horn but he had to set the people straight. So the next day he gave his first campaign speech, launching "into a harangue," he wrote, "in the open air and on a very windy day." It would have been hard for James Madison to pit his small voice against the wind. Many of his words must have blown away, but his harangue worked. He was elected.

The convention was held in June. By this time eight states had ratified. Delaware, New Jersey, Georgia, Connecticut, Maryland, and South Carolina accepted with little trouble. Pennsylvania agreed after a struggle, but Massachusetts argued for a month before it ratified and then only by the narrowest margin—187 votes to 168. If Virginia were the ninth state to ratify, the Union would be safe. If Virginia said No, New York, which was not at all enthusiastic about the Constitution, might follow suit. Then even if nine states did ratify, there wouldn't be much of a union with two of the biggest states out of it.

Because of the crowds, the convention was moved to the largest room in Richmond. Even then it was packed—170 delegates and hordes of spectators, many of them curious to see if Patrick Henry, who was against the Constitution, was really as fabulous a speaker as everyone said he was. He had

Patrick Henry speaking

not given a public speech in twelve years. He was fifty-two years old now and wore a wig which would have covered his baldness if he'd let it. But no, as soon as he got excited, he shoved that wig up and down, back and forth as if it might burst into flames at any minute if allowed to lie still.

His years had not slowed Patrick Henry down one whit. As soon as he stood up, people sighed with satisfaction. Yes, he was the same old spellbinder. He pushed his glasses up on his forehead, raised one shoulder a notch, looked intensely at his audience with what people called his "Patrick flash," and before he said a word, people could sense the entire force of his contempt for the Constitution.

"We the people!" he snorted. Since when had they become "We the *people?*" Were they not still, first and foremost, "We the States" as they had been under the good old Articles of Confederation? And what was wrong with those Articles? Hadn't the people lived in perfect tranquillity under them? Once Patrick Henry spoke eight times in a single day, once he spoke all day long, but no matter how long he spoke or how often, no one moved while he was on stage. During other speeches the audience felt free to shift about and whisper. Stretch their legs. And sometimes leave. It wasn't just what Patrick said that kept everyone so transfixed, it was the way he said it. When he talked of the new government as an empire reducing its citizens to slavery, he raised his arms in such a way that a person could almost see his chains. One member of the audience tested his own wrists to see if they too were shackled. Then there was the time when Patrick pretended to be the state of Virginia, balancing the fate of America on the scales of justice. Eight states were in favor of the Constitution, he said, wiggling those imaginary scales. But what had that to do with justice? If twelve and a half states voted for the Constitution, he cried, still he would "with manly firmness . . . reject it."

No one enjoyed Patrick Henry's theatrics more than Patrick himself, and he had even more reason to be pleased with himself when in the middle of a speech one of his older sons approached the platform with a whispered message. Patrick's wife, Dorothea, had just given birth to Patrick's twelfth child, a boy. There was no stopping Patrick Henry now and no one tried.

When he finally sat down, the Federalists wanted only to get rid of the emotion in the room, set the debate back on firm ground, and let reason take over. But Mr. Madison wasn't the man to do it. Not yet. Let Edmund Randolph start off for the Federalists; he was always impressive. Not until the third day of the debate did James Madison take his turn. He had never faced this many people at one time, but he stood his ground, his hat in his hand, his notes in his hat. He must have expected the audience to walk out because he knew he couldn't be heard in the back of the room and probably not even seen. Sometimes his voice sank so low, not even the secretary recording the meeting could hear it. But people didn't walk out. Those in the back began to move forward and before long much of the audience was standing in front of him, trying to catch his every word. Rocking back and forth on his feet, James Madison poured out his convictions. Firmly, evenly, he talked of checks and balances, pointing out that the Senate, elected by the state legislatures, was really a confederated body while the House, elected by the people, was more national. It was a mixed government. How could it be called an empire, as Mr. Henry had claimed? Only the House had the power to spend money and declare war, and if ever the Congress got out of hand, the President could veto its measures. And if Congress thought the President was wrong, it could over-ride his veto. Where was the slavery in that?

For two days Patrick Henry and other "Antis" attacked the Constitution while James Madison and his friends defended it. Then James Madison took sick with what he called a "bilious attack" and had to go to bed for four days. Others took over for him, and when he came back, James was wearing a brand new buff-colored coat. At least he could be more easily seen now even if he wasn't always heard.

June 26 was the day of the vote. At the last minute Patrick Henry put forward a motion that the Constitution should not be ratified unless all amendments, including a Bill of Rights, should be accepted in advance. Of course this was just another blocking measure. What kind of muddle would they be in, Madison asked, if every state wanted to rewrite the Constitution before it was accepted? He pointed out that the Constitution made provisions for amendments, but Mr. Henry brushed this aside. In one last dramatic stand, he brought God into the argument. "Beings of a higher order," he proclaimed, were watching them this very minute, anxious for justice. Either Patrick was lucky or he had looked out the window, because suddenly, as if on cue, the sky darkened, a storm hit the city, shook the building, and set doors and windows banging and rattling.

James Madison waited out the noise. There was only one question that faced them, he said calmly. It had nothing to do with amendments. It was the Constitution itself. Take it or leave it. Virginia voted to take it. It was a narrow squeak. Eighty-nine votes for ratification; seventy-nine against. Although Virginia would soon learn that New Hampshire was actually the ninth state to ratify, at the moment Virginians believed that they were the ones starting off the Union. Still, there was no celebrating in Richmond that night. The vote had been too close. How could anyone shoot firecrackers over a city where there were so many losers?

Madison went from the convention to Washington's home, Mount Vernon. All during the proceedings he had been writing Washington, keeping him up to date, but now the two men, who had become close friends, would talk over what had happened and discuss the future. Surely Madison must have impressed upon Washington how indispensable he was to the country. Everyone was depending on him to be president and start the government off on the right track. Washington resisted. Truly he wanted nothing more than to spend the rest of his life at his beloved Mount Vernon, but both men knew that in the end Washington would not refuse.

As the summer went on, the Union began to take shape. New York ratified in July and although North Carolina and Rhode Island held back, they were both in the Union not too long after it had formed. Now it was time for Congress to put down on the calendar the dates when the new government would take over.

January, 1789: elections would be held for the presidential electors in each state. Some states would cast more votes than others for the president since the Constitution allows each state the same number of electors as it has senators and representatives. It is these electors who actually cast the vote for their states for president and vice president. (At that time the man who received the most votes from the electors became president while the one with the second most votes became vice president.) February 2: members of Congress would be elected. On March 4 the new Congress would meet in New York; on April 6 it would count the votes for the president and vice president. Later that month the president would be inaugurated.

At first James Madison wanted to be a Virginia senator, but according to the Constitution at that time, senators were elected by their state legislatures, and who controlled Virginia's legislature? Patrick Henry, who in his usual unbridled style declared that James Madison's election would produce "rivulets of blood throughout the land." Indeed, when James decided to run for the House of Representatives, Patrick Henry tried to wreck his chances there too. By deliberately combining Anti-Federalist counties with Orange

County in a congressional district, Mr. Henry hoped to make it impossible for Madison to win.

Madison's friends wrote him in New York, where he was serving in the old, soon-to-be-replaced Congress. Come home, they said. Lies were being spread about him. He would never win unless he spoke up for himself. In other words, electioneer. Just what Madison hated above all else. But when Madison arrived home and heard what was being said—that he opposed adding a Bill of Rights to the Constitution and that he no longer supported freedom of religion—he knew he had no choice. It was not his opponent in the election, James Monroe, who was spreading such stories. Though an Anti-Federalist, Monroe was a close friend, and indeed they traveled together for company as they toured their district, campaigning. Refraining from personal remarks, they stuck to the issues, and Madison must have done well for he won the election by a wide margin. The worst thing that happened to him was that on a bitter cold night, his nose was frostbitten. He carried the scar for life.

On April 6 when the new Congress counted the electoral votes, it was no surprise that George Washington was elected president. John Adams of Massachusetts received the second highest number of votes and became the vice president. Americans had never inaugurated a president before, but they had always known how to put on a show and this was time for one. On April 23 a specially built barge rowed by thirteen men in white uniforms carried the president-elect to Battery Park in New York City. The barge was followed by a mile-long parade of rowboats and sailboats and flying flags, and it was met by explosions of fireworks—rockets shooting into the sky, cascades of stars falling over the harbor, and even a portrait of Washington shot, sparkling, into the air.

In the procession that marched to the actual inaugural ceremony, James Madison was one of five representatives who walked behind Washington and stood nearby throughout the proceedings. Listening to Washington's inaugural address, he would have found no surprises. Washington had shown it to him weeks before and asked what he thought. Too long, Madison said and rewrote it. Later he would write Washington's address to the House of Representatives and then, as if he were carrying on a dialogue with himself, he would write the House's reply to Washington and Washington's reply to the House.

The government was in motion and Madison was obviously close to the helm.

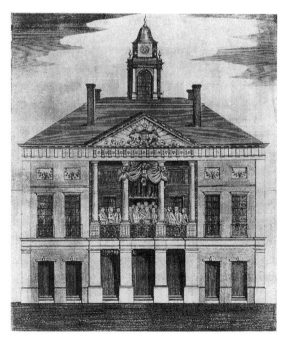

Washington's inauguration at Federal Hall

Five

As Congress began to meet, James Madison wrote to his father: "We are in a wilderness without a single footstep to guide us . . . Those who may follow will have an easier task."

It is interesting that James used the word "may," perhaps not even aware of the edge of doubt he was expressing. Yet no one was sure if this experiment in government would last. Some were frankly skeptical, and some were not afraid to hint that if they didn't get their way, they might just quit and go home. Some acted as if they didn't care. But James would not let himself be discouraged. He took the lead on the floor of the House of Representatives as if he were determined that the government would go on forever or at least as long as he had breath in his body.

He proposed that a Department of War, a Department of

Finance, a Department of Foreign Affairs be established to help the president run executive affairs. He set in motion an act that established a national court system. He had no trouble in carrying these measures, but when he asked for unanimous approval of a Bill of Rights, it was as if he had suddenly bumped into a hornet's nest. This was the bill which people had been crying for, yet here they were abuzz with objections. What was the hurry? some asked. There were more important things to do. Let the Constitution alone; there had been enough trouble about it. Why bother with what a South Carolina representative called "milk and water amendments"? A few, who had still not given up hope for a second Constitutional Convention, plotted for a way to go back and begin over again.

And here was James Madison, who had at first thought a Bill of Rights unnecessary, arguing in its favor. Why? He was just keeping a promise. People who had been promised a Bill of Rights at the ratifying conventions must not be disappointed. Actually, Madison had become convinced that a Bill of Rights was a good idea, not only because it would make people feel safer but because it would help the courts. If certain basic rights were specifically guaranteed (such as freedom of the press, freedom of speech, freedom of religion), the courts would find it easier to protect minorities when they were oppressed by larger, more powerful groups.

Week after week they argued, but the biggest obstacle turned out to be the clause on freedom of religion. "No religion shall be established by law, nor shall the equal rights of conscience be infringed." That sounded too drastic, the representatives said. Did that mean that the states had no say? Worse still, didn't this discourage religion altogether?

No, no, Madison explained. It only meant that no laws could force a person to worship in any way that went against his conscience. In Madison's own mind, religion should be kept absolutely out of government. Later he would oppose taxpayers' money being used for any purpose related to religion. No public land should be given to churches. Congressional chaplains should not be paid from government funds. But now he accepted the final wording, which was limited to the laws that the national government might make. "Congress shall make no law respecting an establishment of religion, or prohibiting the free exercise thereof."

Madison had introduced the Bill of Rights on June 8, but it was not until September 25 that ten final amendments were ready for the president's signature and not until December, 1791, that they were ratified.

But James Madison knew that the real conflicts lay ahead. How were they to raise the money to pay their debts? Where would they put their capital? Every time the subject of the capital came up, James Madison's back stiffened. Not on the Susquehanna River, he said. The climate there was not healthy. And if the fishing was better on the Susquehanna than on the Potomac, what then? Such arguments didn't deserve a reply. Only the Potomac would do. Most centrally located with easy access to the west, it should please everyone. But Madison knew that reason itself was not likely to determine this vote. Perhaps later something would come up and he could make a deal. Perhaps he could give up something he wanted in exchange for the Potomac.

If only Jefferson could have been here in these first "wilderness" days of government! These two good friends had kept up a steady correspondence during Jefferson's stay in France. Jefferson had sent Madison all kinds of books unavailable in America and a variety of gadgets that would appeal to the scientific interests of both men: phosphorescent matches, a pocket compass with a spring that would stop it when not in use, a portable magnifying glass that would fit into a cane and could be taken on walks, a pedometer, a chemistry box. But talk! That's what Madison wanted, so of course he looked forward to Jefferson's return, and indeed it seemed that he might be expected fairly soon. Washington wanted Jefferson to serve as his secretary of foreign affairs (secretary of state, we say today).

But Jefferson was not home in time to help Madison in his most serious confrontation to date. Actually Madison himself was surprised that he would run into trouble with Alexander Hamilton, the secretary of the Treasury with whom he had worked so hard to get the Constitution ratified. They had always been good friends. In the days of the Constitutional debate a little girl remembered watching the two men sitting together in the yard next door, throwing back their heads in laughter as they played with a neighbor's pet monkey.

But this was a new Hamilton who was revealed when he presented his plan for paying the public debt. He wanted to sell government bonds at six percent interest and to redeem old certificates that had been given to veterans for their full value. The trouble was that veterans and others had considered the certificates practically worthless (as they were at the time) and they had sold them for whatever they could get. So who would profit under Mr. Hamilton's plan? Not the veterans but the speculators who had bought up the old certificates. This was not only unfair, Madison said, but it encouraged speculating. Under this plan the rich would get richer, the poor would get poorer, and with public securities built into the money system, the debt would never truly be paid. When it was pointed out that the government's credit would always be good since the government had the power to tax, Madison was still not convinced.

What did this do to the idea of a virtuous little pay-as-you-go republic that Mr. Madison thought they all shared? Then to make matters worse, Hamilton proposed that the national government assume all the debts that the state governments owed, with no allowance for the fact that some states, like Virginia, had already paid off part of their debts. More unfairness, Madison said. A bigger debt. Another incentive to speculators.

When the debate hit the floor of the House, the country learned for the first time that Congress could at a moment's notice turn into a theater. Senators took time off so they could listen to the proceedings. Abigail Adams (wife of the vice president) and her lady friends thronged into the galleries. Alexander Hamilton could not argue his case himself, because he was not a member of the House. Still, it was clearly a fight between two of the country's leaders: Hamilton's supporters on one side, Madison and his men on the other. Spectators looked forward particularly to the times when Mr. Madison spoke. He would shuffle a sheaf of papers, stand up, and clear his throat as if he were alerting the audience that though it might be difficult to hear him, he had something to say. Soft spoken as he was, he tore into Mr. Hamilton's plan as if it offended every nerve in his body. And when he was reminded that this system had worked in England—well, that's when Madison's face reddened and when he began rocking back and forth in his old tense way. Who needed England to show them how to run their country? he would snap. Madison may still have borne old grudges against England, but what he particularly resented now was the way England continued to act as if the United States were a second-rate nation, hardly worth anyone's attention.

On the other hand, when Madison presented *his* plan for raising money, he, too, was shouted down. Why couldn't they sell land in the western territories that would eventually become part of the United States? he asked. George Clymer of Pennsylvania, a follower of Hamilton, snorted at the idea. It was "romantic," he said, to suppose that the western territories would ever agree to come into the United States. Then consider taxes. Consider tariffs, Madison suggested. Why not a whisky tax? Why not a higher tariff on American ships trading with countries having no commercial agreements with us? By this Madison meant Great Britain, which had refused to sign such an agreement, but there was an immediate outcry from New England representatives. They were the ones who did most of the trading with England; they were the ones most partial to their former enemy.

It was toward the end of the debate that Thomas Jefferson arrived back from Paris, back also from a long visit to Monticello, where Madison had seen him over the Christmas holidays. At the first opportunity Hamilton cornered him, explaining how serious the debt problem had become. Particularly the question of the nation taking over state debts. There were some states threatening to secede from the Union, he explained, if the nation did not assume their debts.

Jefferson invited Hamilton to dinner the next night. He would invite Madison too, he said.

By this time Madison realized that he could not win the debate over the funding system. Some of the speculators were themselves members of Congress. Moreover, if the country's money was largely in the hands of those who were wealthy and able to speculate, the stability of the country would be assured. That was what many believed. There remained, however, the delicate question of state debts. Hamilton needed only a few more votes to get his way on this. While Madison had no notion of changing *his* vote, he did agree that he might possibly arrange among his supporters to give Hamilton his victory. *If,* he said. If Hamilton for his part would see that the vote on the location of the national capital went as Madison wanted it. The Potomac River as the permanent site. A ten-year temporary site at Philadelphia. Hamilton agreed.

Still, at the end of the evening James Madison knew that he and Hamilton would never again sit and laugh together over the antics of anyone's pet monkey. He felt betrayed. Perhaps he should have paid more attention to Hamilton's outburst at the Constitutional Convention. Loyal as he was to the American cause, Hamilton, born and brought up on a British island in the West Indies, obviously still held an undue admiration for British aristocracy. He was an ambitious man, Alexander Hamilton, handsome and charming with the ability to manipulate people to do what he wanted them to do. And Madison worried about his influence over President Washington.

Actually Alexander Hamilton may himself have felt betrayed. He and Madison had both promoted the idea of a strong central government, yet in this crucial case Madison did not seem to be behind it. Madison could have pointed out, however, that he had not changed. First and foremost, he was in favor of a balance of power. If one branch of government seemed to be showing too much power, if the central government seemed to be dominating the states, he would always try to tip the scales. A few months later he would oppose Hamilton again when he succeeded in establishing a national bank. Madison advised Washington that the bank was unconstitutional and he shouldn't sign the bill. But Washington listened to Hamilton instead, just as Madison feared. And he did sign the bill.

But all that lay in the future. Right now Madison was so

happy to have Jefferson back and working in the government, he put aside his worries. When Congress adjourned for its summer recess, Madison and Jefferson rode home together, Jefferson stopping off at Montpelier. It is pleasant to imagine these two old friends stopping for á meal of Maryland crabs, admiring the view from a window in the Annapolis steeple, jogging through the Virginia countryside, talking, talking, still making up for all the conversation they had lost. If Madison had not already told Jefferson about the man who in the early days of the administration applied to him for a job, he may have told him now. Or he may have told it again; it was one of his favorite stories. In those days because of his position in the government Madison was besieged by requests for jobs that he had no authority to give. But there was one man who was persistent. He came to Madison, asking for an appointment as governor of a western territory. Madison told him, No, he couldn't help. A few days later the man returned. Could Madison give him a post office job? he asked. Again Madison said no. The man did not give up, yet every time he came back with a new idea, Madison had to turn him down. Finally the man came with one more request. Did Madison have any old clothes he could spare? he asked. Madison never failed to laugh at the incident and would have enjoyed sharing it with his friend.

He enjoyed sharing everything with Jefferson. Even a horse, if that was what Jefferson wanted. And at Montpelier Jefferson did take a fancy to one of Madison's horses. Could he buy it? he asked. Of course. They agreed on the price—twenty-five pounds—and Jefferson took it with him to Monticello. The only trouble was that soon after reaching Monticello, the horse died. Jefferson had not paid for it yet but he insisted he would. Madison said, No, he didn't want anyone paying for a dead horse. But it wasn't dead when he took it, Jefferson replied, and the argument went back and forth until Jefferson finally forced the money on Madison. Arguments over horses could be serious business in Virginia, but not between these two, who could never find it in their hearts to blame each other for anything.

In November Madison and Jefferson accompanied each other to Philadelphia, the temporary seat of the government. Of course they both expected trouble from Alexander Hamilton, whose idea of a republic obviously differed so much from theirs, but they could not have anticipated how the sides would line up in the country, one side backing Hamilton, the other backing Jefferson and Madison. Newspapers joined the battle; indeed, for the next two years that was where the fiercest fighting took place—one Philadelphia newspaper (backing Hamilton) against the other (backing Jefferson and Madison). The editors of both papers were masters in the art of blistering attack, but according to Jefferson and Madison, the editor of Hamilton's paper often resorted to downright lies. Jefferson was the principal target of abuse (perhaps because he was the most likely presidential candidate in the future) but he could not bear controversy. So invariably he would call on Madison to reply to the false accusations. Many of the articles were written under assumed names by Hamilton and Madison themselves, these two men who had once collaborated on the famous Federalist papers.

In September 1792, Madison (writing under his own name at this time) summed up what he saw as the difference between the two sides. Those who were the real friends of the Union, he said, put their faith in the people, resisted measures which suggested tyranny in any form, and were against public debt. Madison called this party the Republican Party, although the term would not apply to present-day Republicans. Indeed it is the Democrats today who trace their roots to Jefferson's and Madison's philosophy, with its theory of spreading power democratically among the people. In the days of the Constitutional Convention, however, no one had thought the country would divide into parties, and even now Madison expected this to be a temporary affair. Madison called Hamilton's party the Anti-Republicans, although many Republicans referred bluntly to the opposition as Monarchists. (They called themselves Federalists.) This party, so Madison claimed, did not trust people to govern themselves. Instead they believed that the only way to keep order and encourage prosperity was to give power to people of "quality," use organized business to support the government and a strong executive and military means to control it.

The only thing that Jefferson, Madison, and Hamilton seemed to agree on was that Washington should serve a second term as president. Washington did not think he could bear it. He dreamed of Mount Vernon as a man stranded in a desert dreams of water. Indeed he went so far as to ask Madison to write a brief farewell statement for him. Reluctantly Madison did, but at the last minute it was Alexander Hamilton who persuaded Washington to change his mind. All right, Washington agreed, but please let there be no more fighting between the men in his cabinet. Hamilton promised but, as time would prove, it was a promise he could not keep.

Actually events themselves made it hard to keep peace within the government. Trouble in Europe reverberated in the United States, as it always would. There was no way, Americans discovered, that they could live in isolation, but at first when the French initiated their own revolution (1789), Americans responded with a burst of enthusiasm. Just look what Americans had started, they cried. The spirit of liberty was spreading over the world. Americans sang the French

Revolutionary song and called each other in the French style "Citoyen" or "Citizen." But the excitement did not last long. In France extremists took control of the Revolution and went on a rampage—beheading the king, killing each other, destroying property, and in general smashing the very ideals they had been promoting. Americans in turn were disillusioned but reacted along party lines. The Federalists said: See? See what happens when the people have power? See how they go wild? The Republicans denounced the French barbarity, but still they could not turn away from France and its desire for liberty.

As for Great Britain, it was alarmed at the way the French extremists were trying to spread their revolution to other countries. A traditional enemy of France, Great Britain did not want the balance of power in Europe upset, nor did it like the idea of kings being toppled off their thrones. So it went to war against France. Again Americans took sides: Federalists lining up with Great Britain, Republicans with France. Washington declared America's neutrality but even this produced arguments. No one wanted America to go to war, but Madison pointed to America's 1778 alliance with France, which pledged mutual help in time of need. Hamilton disagreed. Since the French government had changed, he said, America was no longer bound to old agreements.

In short the country was in turmoil. Journeying back to Philadelphia in the fall of 1792, Madison was not only downhearted about the country, he was lonely. His favorite brother, Ambrose, had just died; his father's health was failing; Jefferson had given notice that he would leave the government at the end of the year; and Washington, as a Federalist, was no longer the close friend he had once been. James Madison was forty-three years old now, and although

James Madison

everyone else seemed to take for granted that he would never marry, Madison himself had made no such decision. He had been so busy, so preoccupied with the government, he had probably not concentrated on the matter. Perhaps he was waiting to fall in love. Perhaps he thought it would just "happen," as it had with Kitty Floyd. But it hadn't happened. If he was ever to marry, he would obviously have to make an effort. And he was ready.

Dolley Madison

Six

I n the fall of 1793 the city of Philadelphia was recovering from the shock of a summer-long epidemic of yellow fever. Before it was over, four thousand people had died and many had fled the city to escape danger. Housewives were either too sick or too busy to wash their doorsteps twice a week as they normally did. And when the watchman went through the streets at ten o'clock in the evening calling "All's well," everyone knew that all was far from well. Those who stayed behind walked in the middle of the street in an effort to avoid contagion. They burned tar and sprinkled their clothes with vinegar, hoping this would keep them safe. Jefferson went to a little resort in the suburbs, Washington returned to Mount Vernon, but Hamilton caught the fever—only a light case, and he recovered rapidly.

Among those who died were Mr. and Mrs. Todd, an elderly couple who had been cared for right up to the end by their lawyer son, John Todd. John had moved his wife, Dolley Payne Todd, their year-old son, Payne, and their brand-new baby to the country before returning to his parents. When they died, he rushed back to Dolley, but by this time he too was sick and died almost immediately. Dolley and the little baby both caught the fever, and although the baby died, Dolley recovered.

When the epidemic was over, Dolley and little Payne ("Precious Payne" she called him) returned to Philadelphia at about the same time as James Madison arrived. James did not know Dolley, but during the next months he undoubtedly heard of her and since she lived just a block from where Congress met, he may even have seen her. She was such a beauty that it was said that men stationed themselves so they could watch her pass. If James too had stationed himself, he would have seen a striking twenty-five-year-old with blue eyes and black hair, dressed in the plain clothes worn by Quakers. She was the same height as James and had such a friendly air about her that James would not have been intimidated. Indeed, possibly through seeing her and certainly through hearing about her, she worked on James's imagination until he was almost persuaded that she was the One.

His chief informant was his old Princeton friend Aaron Burr, who had once lived at the boarding house that Dolley's mother ran and knew Dolley well. The story of Dolley's family was a sad one. Although Dolley's mother had long been a Quaker, her father, John, was converted after his marriage. Once he became a Quaker, however, he was a wholehearted one. Although at that time the Paynes lived on a plantation in Virginia, it went against John's conscience to own slaves and as soon as Virginia made it legal to free them, John Payne freed his, sold his plantation, and moved to Philadelphia where he opened a starch business. But starch was a poor choice. Even in prosperous times he would have had to sell a lot of starch to support a family, and the times were not good. Before long John Payne had to declare bankruptcy. The Quakers, however, disapproved of bankruptcy. They disapproved of all debts, even when they were unavoidable. So they "disowned" John Payne; they no longer allowed him to attend their meetings. He was Out. John Payne was so depressed that he shut himself up in his bedroom and never came out. Two years later he died.

If asked, Aaron Burr would have said, No, he did not think Dolley's Quaker faith would stand in the way of her considering marriage to a non-Quaker. Several of her sisters had married non-Quakers and had been "disowned," but she did not seem overly upset by this. Moreover, she had made Aaron, another non-Quaker, the legal guardian of her Precious Payne. The only negative thing that Aaron Burr could have found to say about Dolley was that she was related to Patrick Henry. Her mother was Patrick's cousin. James would have laughed. If it turned out that he liked Dolley and Dolley liked him, he wasn't going to worry about Patrick Henry.

So in the spring, when Dolley had had enough time to recover from her first grief and before other suitors began beating their way to her door, he asked Aaron Burr to arrange an introduction.

Dolley went into a flurry of excitement as soon as she received the message from Aaron. James Madison, no less! The famous Madison. She couldn't receive him without having another woman present. Dolley's thirteen-year-old sister, Anna, was living with her, but Dolley wanted her best friend, Eliza Collins, to come—not only for the sake of etiquette but to share the excitement. She dashed off a note.

"Thou must come to me. Aaron Burr says that the great little Madison has asked to be brought out to see me this evening."

What to wear? Dolley, who loved bright colors, had never been allowed to wear them because of Quaker restrictions, but she did have a mulberry satin dress, which may have been just within (or perhaps just without) the bounds of the Quaker code. She tied a kerchief to her neck and set a lace cap on her head. There. She was ready.

For his part, Madison bought a new round beaver hat, but in spite of a certain degree of nervousness that they both must have felt, the evening went well. Dolley was a warm person with a natural gift for making people feel at ease, and however she steered the conversation, she must have brought out the kindness and the humor that so often lay hidden under the surface of Madison's personality. In any case, James Madison fell headlong in love, began making regular calls, and within a few months was proposing marriage.

Dolley was not sure. She certainly admired Madison (which is what she always called him). She suspected she could never find a more considerate stepfather for her Precious Payne. But was this enough? In June she told James that she would visit relatives in Virginia while she thought it over. Meanwhile James went home to Montpelier for the summer and waited for her answer. But he didn't remain silent. He encouraged Dolley's cousin Catherine, who lived nearby, to impress Dolley with how much he loved her.

"He thinks so much of you in the day," Catherine wrote Dolley, "that he has lost his Tongue, at Night he Dreams of you and starts in his sleep."

At last in August Dolley wrote Madison that she had made up her mind. The answer was Yes. Madison was exuberant and wrote right back: "I hope you will never have another deliberation. If the sentiments of my heart can guarantee those of yours . . . there can never be a cause for it."

The wedding was on September 15 at the Virginia home of Dolley's sister Lucy, married to George Steptoe Washington, nephew of the president. There is no record of what Dolley wore, but she was obviously no longer going to obey the dictates of the Quaker faith. She had on her finger her engagement ring of rose diamonds and around her neck an elaborate necklace of carved medallions, which James gave her as a wedding present. This was the first jewelry Dolley had ever worn. As a little girl, she had treasured a locket her grandmother had given her in secret since jewelry was forbidden to Quakers, but had kept it hidden and was heartbroken when she lost it. But now since she expected to be disowned, she was free to have the pretty things she had once only admired.

On the day of her wedding, however, Dolley still had mixed feelings. She wrote Eliza Collins just before the ceremony. "In this union I have everything that is soothing and grateful in prospect, and my little Payne will have a generous and kind protector." But she must have still wondered if this was enough. She signed her letter "Dolley Payne Todd," but after the ceremony she added a postscript. "Evening. Dolley Madison! Alass! Alass!" She probably did not regret the step she had taken but she did recognize that there was no turning back. And "Alass!," this was rather scary.

Dolley needn't have worried. The affection she felt for Madison developed gradually into genuine love, and Madison so adored Dolley that he accepted Precious Payne, spoiled and obnoxious as everyone else found him, with more patience than he might have shown a child of his own. (Dolley and James never had children.) Indeed, Precious Payne was a problem all his life, one his mother refused to admit, yet for her sake, Madison never complained. Dolley in turn flung herself enthusiastically into her husband's political career, learning the ins and outs of government, rejoicing in Madison's political victories, grieving over defeats. After some years Dolley described their marriage. "Our hearts understand each other," she wrote.

While the Madisons were on their honeymoon, the United States faced its first small insurrection. The farmers in western Pennsylvania resented the tax that had been placed on whisky. For them it was not a tax on a luxury item; it struck at the source of their income. Since it was impossible to transport the grain they grew over the mountains, they converted it to whisky and sent the whisky East to be sold. Claiming that they had been unfairly discriminated against, they petitioned the government for relief, and when that didn't work, they began tarring and feathering those who opposed them, burning barns, and in general intimidating, eluding, and resisting tax collectors. This was only a brief spurt of rebellion, however, which petered out once the farmers learned that in the East they were being accused of treason.

Like everyone else, Madison disapproved of breaking laws for any reason, but in the end he was more afraid of Alexander Hamilton's reaction than he was of the Pennsylvania farmers. Hamilton seemed to jump at the chance to play the hero. In a brand-new general's uniform, he rode to Pennsylvania with an army of fifteen thousand militiamen as though he were going to conquer the West. The uprising was over by the time he got there, and to the people of Pennsylvania he presented a foolish spectacle—this self-important man rounding up farmers from their fields while his troops tramped down the countryside. In the end he marched twenty so-called ringleaders to Philadelphia, but eventually they were freed and sent home.

What Madison feared was Hamilton's tough talk. If a lesson were not made of these men, Hamilton insisted, the next storm would be worse. The government needed a standing army ready to put down future troublemakers at a moment's notice. And if there was one thing that Madison dreaded more than any other, it was talk of a standing army. Any government with a standing army had more power than could easily be controlled. As far as Madison could see, the Whisky Rebellion was no encouragement to future "storms," as Hamilton would have people believe. It was a warning against them.

But in November, as the Madisons settled down in Philadelphia in their rented three-story brick house, Madison was less troubled by the Whisky Rebellion than he was by Great Britain, which was making it all but impossible for America to remain neutral in the war in Europe. The Royal Navy had been ordered to seize all food on American ships bound for France. And because the British claimed the West Indian ports for their exclusive use, they began capturing American

A tax collector who confiscated two kegs of whisky is followed by two farmers who plan to tar and feather him.

ships found there. They stopped American ships at sea to search for British seamen who might have deserted to join the more lenient American Navy. If they felt like it, they took American seamen as well. Indeed, Great Britain not only disregarded America's sovereignty, it simply did not bother to abide by the peace treaty both nations had signed at the end of the war.

James Madison found this behavior intolerable. Long before his marriage to Dolley, he had introduced a bill placing heavier duties on British goods as a penalty for their hostility. But the Federalists would have nothing to do with Madison's bill. Great Britain would just get mad, they said. Then where would they be? Back at war again. Still, they knew that something had to be done. Washington decided to send an envoy to London to try to negotiate the differences between the two countries. But in the opinion of Madison and Jefferson, he picked the wrong man. John Jay. Like Hamilton, Jay had once worked closely with Madison to secure the ratification of the Constitution; like Hamilton he had turned into a staunch Federalist.

So while Dolley and James started the business of housekeeping, the whole country awaited the outcome of Jay's mission. Rumors seeped across the Atlantic that Americans would not be happy with the results of the negotiation, but it was not until after Congress had adjourned on March 3, 1795, that the actual text of Jay's treaty arrived in Philadelphia. The rumors were correct. No one liked the treaty. There was not a word in it about the capture of American sailors or the searching of American ships, no recognition of America's right to ship food to France, and although American ships were allowed into West Indian ports, there were so many "ifs, ands and buts" to this provision, it was meaningless. In other words, John Jay, always known as an admirer of Great Britain, had come home empty-handed. He may have done the best that he could, but people felt he had sold out.

And they were outraged. They could not believe that the Senate would ratify the treaty, yet the Senate, still afraid of war with Great Britain, did. And Washington signed it. Nothing that happened in postwar America caused such disruption. Rioting broke out in major cities. Stones were thrown at Hamilton when he spoke in defense of the treaty. And John Jay was burned in effigy in so many towns, he said that he could have found his way across the country by the light from the fires.

But James Madison was not ready to give up. He admitted that only the Senate had the right to approve or disapprove a treaty, yet only the House of Representatives had the right to spend money or withhold money. So if the House refused to put certain measures of the treaty into effect, didn't that automatically kill the treaty itself? He argued that rejection of the treaty should not anger Britain; it simply affirmed the independence of the United States. Madison told Jefferson that he felt sure that the Republicans would win the vote on April 29, but, as it turned out, they lost by one vote. The Federalists had fifty votes; the Republicans forty-nine. Madison and Jefferson were shocked at the outcome. If the Federalists were this successful, they said, the Republicans would have to work harder to strengthen their party. The only way to save America, they decided, was to make sure that the Republicans did well in future elections.

Washington waited until September 1796, to make the formal announcement that he would not seek a third term, and since elections were held in November, there was not much time for the Republicans to build up their strength. John Adams would certainly run as the Federalist choice for president and whether Jefferson wanted to or not, the Republicans put his name on their ticket. If he didn't become president this time, he surely would the next time (1800). As for the coming election, the Republicans had little doubt that Jefferson would at least come in second, which would make him vice president.

It worked out just as Madison had anticipated, although he had hoped for more. On March 4, 1797, John Adams was inaugurated president of the United States and Thomas Jefferson became vice president. And James Madison retired from public life. The Federalists scoffed at the news of Madison's retirement. Yes, he'd take some time off, they said, but like Jefferson, he'd be back on the public stage. And indeed it is hard to imagine that Madison seriously believed that he could abandon politics forever. Still, he did look forward to life at Montpelier with Dolley. From Philadelphia he shipped five bushels of clover seed to Montpelier, eighteen chairs, and sixteen boxes and trunks. He and Dolley had so much personal baggage, they had to hire extra horses to carry it all.

Since his father was laid up with rheumatism, James took over the management of the plantation. He had long ago given up the idea that he could manage without slaves, but he never ceased to feel guilty about owning them. One can't help but wonder what he thought of Dolley's father, who freed his slaves and gave up his livelihood rather than betray his principles. Did he admire John Payne for his courage? Or did John Payne simply prove how impractical it was to take such a solitary stand? Much as Madison and Jefferson abhorred slavery, it probably never occurred to them that they could abandon Monticello and Montpelier, and they recognized that it would be impossible to maintain their homes without slaves. Yet even if they could, they had been brought up to believe that ex-slaves would never be able to survive in a white society without being cruelly discriminated against. Later they would come up with the idea that certain territories in the West could be set aside for the settlement of ex-slaves. Or perhaps they could be relocated in Africa. Apparently no one asked the slaves what they thought.

James's one-time scheme of becoming independent by the sale of that Mohawk property he had bought came to nothing. When he sold it in 1796 he had just enough money to put up a grist mill on the plantation. In the business now of fixing up the house, he ordered marble for a fireplace and arranged to buy 50,000 nails handmade at Jefferson's Monticello factory. From Philadelphia he ordered 190 French window panes. Although he seemed to be fully occupied with planting and building, and like any other farmer, watching the weather, his mind, as anyone might have guessed, was seldom far from Philadelphia.

The trouble now was with France. Already angry at the way Jay's treaty favored England, the French were doubly

This chair was made especially for James Madison by Thomas Jefferson.

angry that the Americans had elected a pro-British Federalist as their president. What was more, they took offense at Adams's inaugural address, which they claimed was unfriendly to the French. So they ordered the American minister out of the country and at the same time began harassing American shipping and capturing American goods at sea. As for American seaman found on British ships, they announced that they would hang them as soon as they were captured.

Madison had never liked John Adams, not only because he was a Federalist but because Madison had never tried to understand the man beneath his pompous manner. Anti-French, pro-British he might be, but Adams was not as confirmed a Federalist as Madison imagined him to be. Although he seemed bent on war, neither Madison nor Jefferson realized that it was Alexander Hamilton who was offstage, pulling strings behind Adams's back. Retired from the government, Hamilton was nevertheless in control of the cabinet that Adams had inherited from Washington. When in 1798 a peace mission to France failed, Hamilton began immediately to press for a larger army, more taxes, a stronger navy. Adams was not against preparedness, but he had not given up on peace. He appointed Washington commander in chief of this new army, hoping he would provide some measure of moderation, but when Washington made Hamilton his second in command, Adams felt he was losing all control.

Besides, John Adams was being attacked mercilessly by Republican newspapers. A sensitive man, he found this hard to take, particularly when they made fun of him personally. Most vicious was a Philadelphia paper edited by Benjamin Bache (grandson of Franklin, whom the Federalists nicknamed Lightning Rod, Jr.). Like other Federalists, Adams did not want a war with France and blamed these newspaper attacks on the French, working behind the scenes to weaken the government from inside. Critics, according to the Federalists, were no longer patriotic Americans; they must be French agents. When Benjamin Bache referred to John Adams as "old querilous, Bald, blind, Toothless Adams," Abigail Adams could stand it no longer. As far as she was concerned, this was treason. "Nothing," she declared, "will have an effect on Bache until they pass a Sedition Bill."

Congress apparently agreed. In July 1798, it passed an Alien Act, which allowed the president to deport aliens who were citizens of an enemy nation in case of war or a threat of war. Even more serious was the Sedition Act, which forbade writing or speaking against the government or the president with the purpose of bringing them into contempt. When a Republican congressman published an article in his home-town newspaper describing Adams as greedy, hungry for power, seeking praise, he was taken to court and found guilty.

Here was the most ominous threat yet to the Constitution. Did no one remember, Madison asked, the First Amendment, guaranteeing freedom of speech? Jefferson and Madison, visiting together at Montpelier, agreed that this was an emergency more dangerous perhaps than war itself. The Sedition Act was nothing more, they believed, than a Federalist tactic to silence the Republicans. Moreover, it was a first step toward monarchy. What would the Federalists do next? Sitting on Madison's front porch, watching summer lightning play over the distant mountains, the two men discussed what could be done. They could not depend on courts; the judges were all Federalists. But the states could object. After all, federal power was limited by the Constitution.

So Jefferson went home and wrote the Kentucky Resolves, protesting that the Alien and Sedition Acts were unconstitutional. And Madison wrote the Virginia Resolves. Both sets of Resolves passed the two state legislatures, but Jefferson, apt to be more hot-headed than Madison, went so far as to say a state could actually nullify federal acts it considered unconstitutional. Madison said this was going too far. This suggested that a state had a right to secede from the Union, and that was the worst thing that could happen. What good was the Constitution if it didn't keep the Union together? Jefferson agreed. He had gone too far.

No other state rose to support the Resolves, and indeed as more editors were tried and found guilty, the Federalists seemed to be riding high. In 1799 with the elections only a year off, Republicans rolled up their sleeves, determined to bring the Federalists down.

Did Madison really think he could keep out of politics at this critical point in the nation's development? He said so. When a delegation of Republicans called on Madison to ask him to run for the state legislature, he said No. He said No several times. He had retired. But then he was told Patrick Henry might be running—not to support his principles but simply because he hated Madison and Jefferson so much. Well, in that case, Madison said, he would run. And of course he was elected.

In the following year two important events changed the color of American politics. John Adams, in effect, split the Federalist party. He simply could not stand Alexander Hamilton's meddling any longer, so he fired his cabinet, which Hamilton had controlled. Then he ruined Hamilton's well-laid plans for a war. Secretly exploring peace possibilities with France, he found a way to restore relations. Wrong-headed John Adams might be at times, but he was an independent man, and though he wanted desperately to be reelected, he knew that he might have wrecked his chance.

Still, he didn't regret what he had done. To the day he died he took pride in the fact that he had, almost single-handedly, kept America out of war.

Overshadowing everything, however, was the fact that on December 14, 1799, George Washington died. Of course the people knew this would happen sometime, yet they felt that they had been suddenly robbed of their security. How could they get along without Washington? They went to such extravagant lengths in their mourning, it was as if they hoped to find strength simply by glorifying him. Mock funerals were held throughout the country, statues were built, streets renamed, and newspapers were so busy finding adjectives to apply to Washington ("sainted," "peerless," "revered," "heroic," "immortal") that they scarcely had time to talk about the coming election.

The Federalists put up Adams for president and Charles Cotesworth Pinckney for vice president. The Republicans put up Jefferson for president and Aaron Burr for vice president. The understanding was clear in both parties just which man was meant to be president and it was expected that the electors would not split their votes. But behind the scenes Hamilton, who hated Adams, was plotting for Pinckney to receive more votes. And Aaron Burr in an underhanded way was plotting for his own victory. If it had all worked out the way Burr planned, he would have been elected president. But at the last minute the New York elector who had promised to keep Jefferson's name off his ballot was prevented from doing so by other Republican electors. The result was that Jefferson and Burr were tied for the presidency. The Constitution had provided for such an emergency. In the case of a tie, the House of Representatives would decide between the two candidates.

In the beginning Burr made generous-sounding statements

A portrait of the "sainted" Washington
ascending into heaven

that he would step aside because of course the Republicans had meant to elect Jefferson, but he said nothing officially. So on February 11 the House of Representatives voted. And voted again. And again. After three days and thirty-two ballots the vote was still tied. Finally on the thirty-fourth ballot Thomas Jefferson was declared the president of the United States. As for Aaron Burr, he might be vice president, but whether he knew it or not, his political career was finished. Neither the Federalists nor the Republicans trusted him. And certainly Dolley and James didn't.

James Madison commented on the election: Wasn't it lucky that the country didn't have a standing army? In another country an army might have been used to seize power. But in spite of political maneuvers, the Constitution had worked. And now Madison knew that he too was headed back into the thick of government. In the early days of the campaign he had promised that if Jefferson was elected, he would serve in his cabinet as secretary of state.

James and Dolley had hoped to attend Jefferson's inauguration on March 4, but in the last week of February James's father died. Because James needed to take care of his father's affairs and because he was himself ill, James was kept at Montpelier for almost two months. But on May 1, 1801, leaving the flowering redbuds behind, the Madisons arrived in the half-built capital at Washington, D.C., ready to take up a new life. For Madison this meant a new chance for America. Working together, surely he and Jefferson would be able to swing the country back into line, establishing it firmly on republican principles.

Seven

In the seventeenth century a man named Francis Pope had been one of the first owners of the land on which Washington, D.C. was now being built. He must have had a sense of humor, for he called his property Rome and named the little stream that ran through it the Tiber after the famous Roman River. All this was just so he could be addressed as "The Pope of Rome on the Tiber." By the time the capital city was established, Mr. Francis Pope had of course been long dead, but the little Tiber was still there, running in swampy ground between the president's house and the Capitol. In time the Tiber would be diverted, lose its name, and be replaced by what is known as Pennsylvania Avenue. Yet when Jefferson took office the city was still a semiwilderness with some shacks and a few fine houses scattered through the woods, while most of its streets were still in the planning stage.

President Jefferson did not in the least mind the disorderly scene of frantic construction that was going on all about him. Forever pulling down, putting up, and redesigning Monticello, he was used to living in clutter and was excited to think that a whole city was being dug out, built up, and hammered together around him. Unlike John and Abigail Adams, who found the president's unfinished Mansion (or Palace as it was often called) cold and uncomfortable, Jefferson said it was a "very agreeable country residence." As president, he planted a double row of poplar trees up swampy Pennsylvania Avenue and built a rough sheep fence around the Mansion.

More important, Jefferson changed the style of life inside his Mansion. No more ceremonial folderol for him. No

President's Mansion

weekly high-toned receptions such as Washington and Adams had held. Determined to put a republican stamp on his administration, he shocked many people by refusing to act as a head of state. Unattended by servants, he walked or rode horseback around town instead of riding in a carriage as all dignitaries did. When senators or congressmen called, Jefferson often met them in his old bedroom slippers with holes in the toes. Sometimes his hair wasn't even properly combed; often his pet mockingbird was perched on his shoulder, looking over the company as if he expected to give his report on the meeting later. When it came to state dinners, Jefferson paid little attention to proper seating arrangements, letting ambassadors and their wives sit any old place as if there were no rules for guests of honor. He made a lifelong enemy of Mrs. Merry, the wife of the British ambassador, and when he was asked what etiquette he followed, he answered, "pell-mell."

When the Madisons first arrived in Washington, they lived with Jefferson in the President's Mansion for a short time. After the summer recess they moved two blocks away into a three-story brick house which boasted a cupola on its roof with a fire escape. The Madisons, however, did not feel the need to create quite as republican an image as Jefferson had. Although James stuck to his usual black breeches with knee buckles and laced shoes, he had no objection to Dolley indulging in fancier tastes. And Dolley, freed from Quaker restrictions, had discovered shopping. Whether she was buying furnishings for Jefferson's household or for her own or clothes for Jefferson's two married daughters (who visited from time to time) or clothes for herself, it didn't matter. She simply loved to shop. Deprived of pretty clothes for so long, she especially liked to buy stylish dresses, often with the help of the French minister's wife. Dolley became partic-

One of Dolley's dresses

ularly partial to the Empire style when it became fashionable—low-necked, high-waisted, and sleeveless. Later she would be known for her turbans. All kinds of turbans—satin, silk, plumed, flowered, she collected them all. Indeed, over the years she became so famous for high fashion that the first question women would ask after a Washington party was: What did Mrs. Madison wear?

Yet it was not her clothes but her warm personality that made Dolley popular. She carried herself like a queen, people said, yet she was so natural, she created an atmosphere of easy friendship and lively conversation wherever she went. James too was more sociable than he'd been. Ever since his marriage, people noticed, he had seemed more relaxed. He was quicker to laugh and although he had always loved good stories, he told them more frequently now and, as everyone agreed, no one told a story better than he did. In short, Washington society could always count on a good time when invited to the Madisons' home. Only Mrs. Merry complained. Once after an ample dinner, which included beef soup, cabbage, ham, and apple pie baked in the form of a muskmelon, Mrs. Merry grumbled. It was more like a "harvest-home dinner," she said, than what one would expect at the table of the secretary of state. When Dolley heard this, she laughed. Why not? she said. The country had an abundance of food, why hold back?

But of course it was not only Republican style but Republican politics that was on trial. Jefferson, Madison, and a loyal Republican Congress wasted no time in letting the country see that they meant to put in practice what they had been preaching all these years. Congress did away with internal taxes, cut down the national debt, and released all those outspoken Republicans who had been victims of Mr. Adams's Sedition Act. Indeed, the main difficulties the country had faced had been forced on it by foreign wars, but if the country could keep free of entanglements, Jefferson and Madison hoped they would have a chance to make the republican experiment work. At first they were lucky. Right in the beginning of Jefferson's administration (November 1801), England and France made peace with each other. This did not mean, however, that all of Europe was at peace. Over the years while France had been fighting first one country and then another, a general had emerged as a hero to the French nation. Napoleon Bonaparte, hot for conquest, established himself as head of the French government. And although England, tired of war, made peace with him, who knew what to expect with a man like Napoleon on the loose?

But at least with England and France no longer at war, travel across the ocean should be safer. After all, freedom to trade was what Jefferson and Madison wanted above all else—not only freedom on the Atlantic Ocean but freedom on the Mississippi River. Here there could be trouble. What if Napoleon decided to interfere on the Mississippi River? He had a good chance to do this. Spain, which had become a vassal state of Napoleon's, had ceded the Louisiana Territory to France, so if he wanted to, Napoleon could move right into New Orleans at the mouth of the Mississippi River. That would be the end of all freedom of trade on the Mississippi. Besides, who wanted a French colony planted in our own western territory? If that happened, Jefferson said, America would have to do an unthinkable thing: it would have to ally itself with Great Britain. Only Great Britain had a navy strong enough to fight France. The very thought was scary.

So Jefferson came up with the idea of trying to buy Louisiana from Napoleon. He didn't suppose he'd succeed, but just in case, Madison, as secretary of state, sent James Monroe and Robert R. Livingstone to France to try to negotiate a deal. As it happened, Napoleon wasn't nearly through conquering; he wasn't even through fighting Great Britain. (That war was resumed in May 1803.) But he was running short of money and his army in Santo Domingo was being ravaged by disease and defeat. So he was quite pleased with the idea of selling Louisiana. Of course there was some bargaining, but in the end Napoleon was happy that he was getting fifteen million dollars for an out-of-the-way piece of property that he never expected to see. And Americans were jubilant to hear that they had acquired not only New Orleans but 828,000 square miles of territory at a cost of less than one penny an acre. And all without a war!

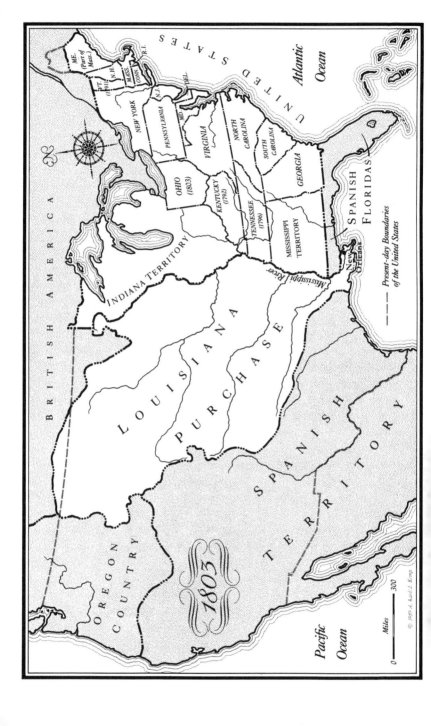

The news of the agreement arrived in Washington on the evening of July 3, 1803, just in time for the Fourth of July. Guns went off at dawn the next morning and President Jefferson threw the Mansion open to the public, many of whom stayed all day and all night to celebrate. Indeed all over the country people continued to celebrate for months. Jefferson knew that to make the Louisiana Purchase entirely legal, he would have to introduce a constitutional amendment and then wait for the amendment to be passed by the states. But suppose Napoleon changed his mind in the meantime? Congress agreed that it couldn't take that chance, so on October 20, 1803, it completed the agreement. In December the Stars and Stripes were raised over New Orleans.

Some Federalists, however, were not happy about the Louisiana Purchase. In New England, some feared that the Louisiana Purchase would give more power to the West and the South; the East would be overshadowed. Besides, they didn't like the way the Republicans were turning the country into what they called a "vulgar democracy." They made fun of all the tough Western characters who would one day be coming into the Union. "Thick-skinned beasts will crowd Congress Hall," Josiah Quincy of Massachusetts grumbled. "Buffaloes from the head of the Missouri and alligators from the Red River." A few Federalist leaders in New England began talking secretly of seceding from the Union if they could find strength enough to support a separate government.

In Virginia, John Randolph, a staunch Republican, also complained about the growth of the country. Only a small republic could maintain its liberty, he said, but John was an eccentric man who was forever disapproving of something. As time went on, he would take Patrick Henry's place in James Madison's life, although he never got under James's skin quite as much as Patrick had. Still, John was a flaming

John Randolph

orator with a flashy style and a shrill voice, and he hated Madison. He insisted that Madison had forsaken Republican ideals. With John Randolph, if something was not a total success, it was a total failure—no changes or compromises allowed. To show that he was still loyal to the original ideals of the party, Representative Randolph called himself an Old Republican. And he was impossible to ignore. He would stride into Congress on his long, stiltlike legs, cracking a riding whip, and followed, often as not, by one of his hunting dogs, as if he were closing in for a kill. Later, in Madison's administration, Dolley would attend a session of Congress if Randolph was going to speak. It was like going to a show, she said.

At the moment, however, no one worried about John Randolph or the Federalists breaking up the Union. The Louisiana Purchase was generally so popular that Jefferson had no trouble being elected for a second term. Governor George Clinton of New York replaced Aaron Burr as vice president and James Madison continued as secretary of state. But it was hard to keep the nation on a steady course. Americans had once believed that the Atlantic Ocean was so wide, it would keep the country safe from European conflicts, but it didn't work out that way. With England and France fighting each other, the Atlantic Ocean became the center of danger. Again England was stopping American ships at sea and kidnapping American seamen under the pretense that they were deserters from the British Navy. It was intolerable, Americans said. Would England never accept the fact that the United States was an independent nation? With each incident Madison and Jefferson protested and at the same time tried every scheme they could think of to get the British to sign an agreement to stop impressment. But the British would do no such thing.

They needed sailors. And that was that. At one point the British foreign minister observed that the idea that the "American flag should protect every Individual sailing under it on a Merchant ship" was too ridiculous even to consider.

Madison and Jefferson could not go on simply protesting, yet they certainly did not want to go to war. The country was just getting on its feet; how could they risk the success of their whole experiment? So they played for time, hoping against hope that the European war would end before they were dragged into it.

But life never operates on just one level at a time. For Dolley Madison, one of the happiest (and yet saddest) events of these years occurred shortly before Jefferson was reelected as president. Her sister Anna Payne, who had lived with her ever since Dolley's first husband, John Todd, died, was to be married to a Massachusetts congressman. The ceremony took place on March 20, 1804, in the Madisons' drawing room, with James Madison giving away the bride. Of course Dolley revelled in all the shopping required for a wedding and in the festivities surrounding it, but it was hard to lose Anna. Indeed, in spite of her active social life, Dolley was for a while inconsolable. Anna was gone; James was so busy, he was out of the house much of the time; and Precious Payne was away at school. He was twelve years old now, more handsome than ever, and if he seemed selfish and irresponsible to others, Dolley paid no attention. How could her Precious Payne not turn out well?

But the world turned too fast for Dolley to waste time feeling sorry for herself. Suddenly the whole nation was shocked by news of a duel between two of its most prominent patriots. Aaron Burr, who had lost his run for governor of New York, blamed his defeat on Alexander Hamilton. It was not the first time he had been angry at Hamilton. He also claimed that Hamilton had been responsible for his defeat as president when the vote had been tied. Behind the scenes Burr had been secretly plotting with a little group of rabid New England Federalists to try and draw New York into their secessionist scheme if he won this election as governor. But he did not win. And Alexander Hamilton, Federalist though he was, had no use for secessionist talk and no use for Aaron Burr. "A despicable person," he called him. "A dangerous man." He didn't care if Burr heard what he said or not, and Burr did hear and didn't like it. He challenged Hamilton to a duel, and although Hamilton didn't believe in dueling, he felt in all honor he had to accept the challenge. He apparently had no intention, however, of pulling the trigger on his gun, no matter what the outcome. When the duelists met on July 11, 1804, on the banks of the Hudson River in New Jersey, the outcome was just what Hamilton must have foreseen. While Hamilton held his fire, Burr did what he'd come to do. He shot and killed Alexander Hamilton.

The outcry across the country, among both former friends and former foes, was unanimous and intense. Burr was called far worse names than any Hamilton had ever used. "You have already heard no doubt of the terrible duel and poor Hamilton," Dolley wrote her sister Anna. She must have wondered how she had ever trusted the guardianship of her Precious Payne to Aaron Burr. In New Jersey Burr was indicted for murder, so he dared not even step into that state, but he had no compunctions about returning to Washington, where he resumed his duties as vice president as if nothing had happened. He knew that when Jefferson's term expired in March 1805, he would not be elected vice president again and would probably never be elected to a public office. But there were other ways to acquire power. "A dangerous man,"

Duel between Alexander Hamilton and Aaron Burr

Hamilton had called him, and already he may have been hatching dangerous plans.

As Jefferson's second term progressed, storms threatened on the horizon, moved in, backed off, and moved in again. England simply would not leave American shipping alone. To justify its action, England quoted an old rule which denied the right of neutral nations to trade with colonies of her enemies. This would keep America out of the West Indies, a principal trading center. England herself, however, kept right on trading with her enemy colonies, so where was the sense in it? Madison, a man who believed that rules should make sense, thought that perhaps he might persuade England to see how unreasonable the rule was, so he wrote a pamphlet filled with legal and historical arguments—a long, wordy essay, a copy of which he sent to England and which he also gave to each United States senator.

A few praised it; most found it boring; John Randolph threw it on the floor of the Senate, calling it a "miserable card-house of an argument which the first puff of wind must demolish." As for England, an anonymous writer claimed that everything Madison had said was wrong. Reason was not going to stop England from doing whatever it wanted to do.

In the spring of 1806 three British warships raided American ships in America's own waters, killing one seaman in the process. The president ordered the three ships to leave America and stay out of all American ports in the future. By 1807 at least two American ships were being seized every week. Then Napoleon declared a blockade of Great Britain and began confiscating American ships and goods. Great Britain said it would take the same measures against neutral shipping that France did.

War was in the air, but in the midst of these difficulties, a plot was developing within the United States itself to break up the Union. In the spring of 1806 Jefferson and Madison began hearing rumors that Aaron Burr had been soliciting money from England, was building boats and gathering an army so that he could take New Orleans. Presumably his purpose was to establish an independent state, perhaps attack Mexico, perhaps even draw the Southern states into a new nation. Madison and Jefferson were appalled at such rumors but knew they had to wait for more evidence. It came the following year, in the spring of 1807. A fellow conspirator, commander of the U. S. Army in the Mississippi Valley and governor of Upper Louisiana, decided that he'd do better telling on Burr than going along with him. The details of what actually took place are still not entirely clear, but Jefferson had heard enough. He was going to catch this Aaron Burr who had wanted to cheat him out of the presidency and was trying now to break up the Union. In March Burr was arrested on the Mississippi River and taken under guard to Richmond to be tried by Chief Justice Marshall. Because Marshall was a Federalist, many did not trust him to hold a fair trial, but fair or not, he ruled there was not enough evidence to prove that Burr was guilty. The rest of the country could believe what it wanted, but there was no proof, Marshall said, that Burr had been present at the time and place the army was being assembled or that the army was gathering for the *express* purpose of making war. Without even hearing all the witnesses, Marshall let Aaron Burr go. And go he did—as fast as he could—to Europe.

Meanwhile England seemed to be actually inviting America to go to war. On June 22 an English ship, the *Leopard,* followed the brand new American frigate, the *Chesapeake,* out of its home port, demanding to search the ship. The *Leopard* surely expected the *Chesapeake* to refuse and of course it did, but the *Chesapeake* did not expect the *Leopard* to open fire. The result was that three Americans were killed, eighteen wounded, and four seamen impressed (only one of whom was actually a British deserter). The *Chesapeake* had to strike her colors, which was a blow to American pride, but even worse, the *Leopard* turned around and anchored within sight of the Virginia coast. Just as if it were thumbing its nose at America.

Jefferson immediately proclaimed that American waters were off-limits for all British ships. He demanded that England apologize, that the captured seamen be returned and that impressment end. The understanding was that if these conditions were not met, war would almost surely follow. Jefferson mobilized 100,000 militiamen to show that America meant business.

But Great Britain was not easily scared by the United States. In December George the Third, who had never recovered from losing his colonies, issued orders to continue impressment. Every neutral vessel bound for Europe, he declared, must stop first in England for a license. France jumped on the bandwagon. Any neutral vessel stopping first in England would be considered fair game for capture.

There was only one alternative, Jefferson and Madison decided. America would keep all its ships at home. Not only would this keep them out of danger, but surely England and France would back down once they began losing money as trade stopped. If reason didn't work, money might. So in December 1807, the United States passed the Embargo Act. No more trade with Europe.

Madison knew that as a result of the Embargo Act Americans as well as Europeans would lose money, but if they went to war, they would lose a great deal more. Surely, Madison thought, Americans would understand this and would stick together. New Englanders were the hardest hit. Their ships lay at anchor up and down the coast, sailors loafed on waterfronts, fish rotted in fish houses, and maritime industries stood idle. And Federalists in New England were furious. Left alone, their ships could at least have gone to Portugal or some other uninvolved country and then traded with England on the sly. They were willing to take their chances but instead they were being treated like children. Was this the freedom they had fought for? they asked. Freedom of the government to reach into their pockets?

In this cartoon about the embargo, the turtle
represents oppression. The smuggler's word "Ograbme"
is "embargo" spelled backwards.

Freedom to rob them of their livelihood? The Embargo Act
was as arbitrary, they claimed, as anything England had
done in the old days. Some even accused Jefferson, who had
been such a friend to France, of wanting to help Napoleon
by ruining American commerce. Some refused to obey the
law, sneaked their ships out of hidden coves at night, and
traded as usual. A few extremists, those who called themselves High Federalists, whispered that New England would
always be discriminated against by the national government;
perhaps it should secede.

People were not only tense about the Embargo Act, however; they were tense about the coming election. For a year
before the actual election they were arguing about who
should be the next president. Although Vice President Clinton had a few supporters, he was generally considered, at
sixty-eight, to be too old. James Monroe had the enthusiastic
endorsement of John Randolph and some of his friends,

largely because Randolph could not bear the idea of Madison becoming president. If Madison were elected, Randolph predicted, "we are gone forever." Madison was criticized for being too weak and he was criticized for being too strong. He was criticized for being a puppet of Jefferson and he was criticized for being Jefferson's master. Yet in the end people seemed to agree that Madison would most likely be the next president.

On March 1, 1809, the Embargo Act, an obvious failure, was repealed and would officially become effective on March 15, two weeks after the inauguration. Foreign armed ships, however, were still excluded from American ports, as well as English and French imported goods. Still, if either England or France gave up its anti-American policy at sea, they were told, America would resume trade immediately. It was another temporary delaying tactic. If there was a solution, it could only be reached by the next administration.

On December 7, the electoral college cast its votes but the result was not officially announced on the floor of the House of Representatives until late February. Spectators crowded into the gallery, waiting to hear the outcome. At the end of two long hours the president of the Senate announced that James Madison would be the new president of the United States. George Clinton would be the vice president.

Everyone knew that James Madison faced critical days ahead, perhaps even war. John Adams was one among many who believed that a second war with England was inevitable. And many wondered about Madison. Described once as a "schoolmaster dressed for a funeral," James didn't look like a leader, certainly not a war leader. Could this little man handle the big job he'd been given?

Eight

On the morning of Madison's inauguration, March 4, 1809, guns were fired at sunrise from both the Navy Yard and nearby Fort Warburton to announce to the nation that this was a special day. Dolley Madison may already have been awake and right away she would have noticed that it was a nice day. The weather would not interfere with the splendor of the festivities.

Affectionately called the "Queen Elect," Dolley had worked hard to get ready for this day. Among all the preparations, there was of course the matter of clothes. For the morning Dolley would wear a long-trained dress of fine white cotton (she would always wear white on state occasions) and on her head she would have a white plumed bonnet. In the evening her gown would be plain buff-colored velvet, but her turban would be a confection of velvet and satin topped with the waving feathers of a bird of paradise. Dolley looked forward to every minute but for James, she knew, the day would be long and hard.

Shortly before noon Dolley and James stepped into their fancy chariot with silver M's blazing on each door. Down Pennsylvania Avenue they rolled, through throngs of people to the Capitol, where ten thousand more people were gathered. Inside the House of Representatives, where the ceremony was to take place, every inch of space was occupied with still more people while senators, justices of the Supreme Court, and the diplomatic corps lined up on the stage with the representatives seated immediately below. All had their eyes on James Madison. For James, who had long ago dedicated his life to forming and upholding the Constitution, it was indeed a grave moment. And scary. He was pale; his hands trembled, and he must have wondered if his voice

**Bust of
Dolley Madison**

would be equal to the occasion. At first he could only manage a whisper but in a few moments he was back in control. In a steady voice, low but audible, he took the oath and gave a ten-minute address in which he summed up his foreign policy. Peace with justice as long as possible; war if the nation's honor was at stake.

When the ceremony was over, the Madisons held open house in their own home since Jefferson had not yet moved out of the President's Mansion. Standing in the doorway, Dolley had never been a more gracious hostess, but James was soon worn out with bowing. People often remarked on the low, formal bow James gave to departing company—as if he were in dancing school, they said. Moreover, in every exchange he always made sure that he was the last to return a bow. And today it seemed he was bowing to every last man and woman in Washington.

Yet more bowing lay ahead in the evening. John Adams and Jefferson had not held inaugural balls as President Washington had, but the Madisons decided to reintroduce the custom. Perhaps they believed it would be politically popular; perhaps Dolley simply insisted that it would be fun. As it turned out, this affair was the most crowded of the day. Long's Hotel, where it was held, was not big enough, but still the people packed in until there was not enough air to breathe. When someone tried to open the windows, it was found that they were painted shut. A few people fainted and then the windows were broken to let in air. Dolley, however, had no intention of fainting. Her plumes waved brilliantly through it all, but James sighed. "I would rather be home in bed," he told a friend.

On March 11 the Madisons moved into the President's Mansion. The fact that it needed redecorating undoubtedly pleased Dolley. What fun it would be to give this official residence the elegance it deserved! Yellow satin curtains in one room. Red velvet at four dollars a yard for the drawing room. In the new State Dining Room she hung portraits of the three former presidents, with a life-size portrait of George Washington at one end. (The frame was so heavy, it had to be nailed to the wall.) And in spite of the expense— $2,150, she bought three large mirrors. She loved mirrors and counted on them to make the rooms seem larger than they were. Particularly the drawing room where she would hold weekly receptions (levees, they were called). She gave her first one on May 31, but it was so well attended (as all her receptions would be) that not even with the mirror could she pretend that the room was large enough.

People began to know what to expect at entertainments at the President's Mansion. No pastry, ever. But they could look forward to being served ice cream, that delicious frozen dessert that Jefferson had introduced from France. Almonds, raisins, pears, apples, peaches would be passed around in baskets. If there was candy, it would be wrapped in paper on which a verse was written. Sometimes they would play cards. For all her Quaker background, Dolley was not afraid to adopt the ways of the world. Always she carried a gold enamel snuff box in her hand. Aaron Burr had deplored this

Dolley's snuff box

habit of hers. Dolley was still pretty, he said, "but oh that unfortunate propensity to snuff-taking." Before long Dolley acquired a parrot. It was something she'd wanted ever since she had been a girl, but to Quakers a pet parrot was considered frivolous. This parrot was surely frivolous, and what was more, it used bad language. Dolley didn't mind. Indeed, every time the parrot swore, she and James laughed.

But people noticed that often at Mrs. Madison's receptions, the president simply stood in the middle of the room, looking distracted. Dolley noticed too and her heart went out to him. She knew what the trouble was. England and France. It was as if these two warring countries had moved into James's mind and taken it over. Nothing had improved since the removal of the embargo. England continued to dictate just where American ships could and could not go, what they could and could not do, and when the English needed more sailors, they stopped American ships and took them. Madison twisted and turned under the insults, for they *were* insults. He protested, threatened, and tried one diplomatic maneuver after another. Why couldn't England see reason?

Occasionally there were moments of hope. Indeed shortly after the inauguration, the British ambassador, David Erskine, told Madison that England was ready to sign an agreement to remove all restrictions on trade. Of course the country was overjoyed and on June 10, 1809, the day trade was officially reopened, the country celebrated in its usual rollicking fashion. Madison had no reason to think that anything would go wrong with the agreement. Still, he had inserted a clause into the agreement reminding King George that he had done nothing to that English officer responsible for firing on the *Chesapeake*. Madison wanted to keep the record straight, and Americans did indeed resent England's ignoring the incident as if it had never happened. But when King George read the clause, he was furious. He would not put up with such impertinence, he said. The deal was off. Forget it. And he recalled his ambassador to the United States, claiming that he had disobeyed instructions. Americans learned the news just ten days after their premature celebration. So it went throughout Madison's administration. Governing the United States was like running an obstacle course, knowing that one misstep could land the country in war. The Federalists were one of the obstacles. They called Madison weak, wavering, pro-French, and entirely dependent on the advice of Jefferson. One Federalist, who kept an eye on Virginia mail, reported that in the course of three months Madison had written to Jefferson twelve times. This proved, he said, that Madison couldn't make a move without Jefferson's approval. (Actually they had been corresponding about problems with a newborn lamb.)

Another obstacle lay with the three British ambassadors who, one by one, succeeded David Erskine. The first was known in Europe as a "hatchet man" and indeed he did seem to approach every problem as if he had a hatchet in hand. Hardly had he arrived in America before he began to talk of exchanging "blow for blow." Finally he became so hostile that Madison told him to go home. The next two ambassadors underestimated Madison and the temper of the country. There would never be war, they said; all this talk by the Republicans was simply political propaganda to help them win the next election. These ambassadors may have been influenced by Federalists, but like many people, they may have been misled by Madison's mild manner. The English government, however, was willing to believe them. After all, as one member of Parliament said, America could not shave itself or catch mice without England's help. Of course America had caught General Cornwallis at the end of the Revolutionary War and he was no mouse. But England seemed determined to overlook General Cornwallis and the Revolutionary War. While France's injustices were due to Napoleon's greediness, Madison said, England's were calculated to keep America weak. America might not be a colony now but it must not become a rival. Madison tried to play one country against the other. If one country would revoke its acts of discrimination against American trade, America promised to give the other country three months to do the same. If the second country did not comply, America would renew its Non-Intercourse Act against it.

In August 1811, there was a flurry of hope when France did revoke its decree with the provision that England would do the same. But England did not. They seemed not to care one way or another about the Non-Intercourse Act. But Americans did. They realized what England apparently did not: The Non-Intercourse Act made war all but inevitable. New England Federalists (always partial to England) cared most of all. They were the ones who did the most trading with England and war was the last thing they wanted. They attacked Madison so viciously in the press that friends suggested that Madison take legal action, but he said No. However history may judge Madison on his political performance, no one can say that he did not stand up for freedom of the press and freedom of religion whenever he had the chance.

Fortunately, summers gave the Madisons a long vacation from Washington and its problems. This year (1811) when the trouble with England was reaching its climax, James and Dolley looked forward eagerly to their time at Montpelier.

Never mind that New England Federalists were threatening to impeach Madison. Next year there would be an election and if the people wanted to get rid of James, they could vote him out. James and Dolley were not going to bother themselves with the Federalists. Or thoughts of the election. They were going to give England every chance to come to its senses, and since it took six or more weeks for news to travel across the Atlantic, they figured that at least their summer was safe.

As soon as Madison had been elected president, he had begun work on remodeling Montpelier. He added two new

Montpelier

wings, one on each side (one so that his mother would have her own suite). He added basement kitchens, a library upstairs, and in the front garden a gazebo, which looked like a small Greek temple. At one point he wrote to Jefferson, asking how to make stucco. When he found out, he had the brick exterior of the house covered with stucco and Dolley had the three front doors painted her favorite color—yellow. One room in the house James called the Clock Room because of the tall English clock that kept time on history itself, for this was also the American History Room. Busts of Washington, Jefferson, John Adams, and others stood around the sides of the room, and portraits of American heroes and pictures of patriotic events hung on the walls. There was also a marble bas relief of Madison, himself. He didn't think of himself as a hero, but he could not deny that the life of the country had long ago also become his own.

Dolley spoke of this summer as being one of "health and peace" which shows how much she enjoyed company. The Madisons were inundated with guests that summer—some invited, some unannounced, but as far as Dolley was concerned the more, the merrier. Both in Washington and here, her sister Anna and her sister Lucy and their children often came for long periods. At one point there were twenty-three children in the house. Dolley laughed. There was plenty of room, and she and James took special joy in their nieces and nephews. But always Dolley had to count on unexpected visitors. Before serving dinner at four o'clock, Dolley or James would look through the telescope that they kept on the front porch to see if anyone was driving up the road. Everyone could expect a warm welcome; the prevailing mood at Montpelier, a guest reported, was one of freedom.

But Congress was to meet in November and nothing was safe after that. Jefferson, who was not a good public speaker, had established the practice of sending his messages to Congress to be read by the clerk, instead of delivering them himself. Madison followed his example. On November 5 his speech was read by a clerk, and no matter how poorly it may have been presented, no one could mistake the urgency of Madison's message. Since war seemed inescapable, Madison said, they should not just wait for it to come; they should prepare for it. In the end Congress agreed that all naval vessels should be made ready for duty and merchant vessels should be armed. More important, a bill was passed to enlist twenty-five thousand men into the army. Even though everyone knew that America didn't have the money to either pay or equip that many troops, the fact that Americans were taking such measures ought to impress England. The news would be sent to England on the ship the *Hornet,* and although they could not expect the *Hornet* to return with a reply before April, they would be preparing for the worst.

The worst was what they expected. Dolley told her sister Anna, "I believe there will be a war," and while there was still time, she wrote to a friend in Paris, asking her to send "large head-dresses, a few flowers, feathers, gloves, stockings—black and white and anything else pretty." But she worried about James. Unable to sleep, he kept his candle lit all night while he read and planned how to carry on the war. Once war was declared, he thought, the best thing to do was to send a small army to Halifax and Quebec before the British could get reinforcements there. In that way, Canada would be held hostage.

But all depended on the *Hornet.* As soon as the trees began to leaf in the spring, people began watching for its return. Perhaps England would reach a quick decision; perhaps the ship would make a fast crossing. At the end of March another ship from England did bring unofficial news.

England was going to keep right on searching American ships and was preparing to send troops to Canada. That was enough for Madison. On April 1 he called for the embargo of all American ships. Those in port should stay there. Those at sea or at foreign ports would have ninety days to get home. Then if nothing had changed, there would be war.

But there was no need to wait ninety days. On May 19 the *Hornet* arrived and all hopes for peace vanished. From the official dispatches it was clear that England had not changed its position and was not willing even to consider change. Everyone knew the next step. According to the Constitution, it was up to Congress to declare war and on June 1 James Madison sent a message to the House, recommending that it do so. On June 4 the House passed a bill to declare war; on June 17 the Senate agreed to it. The next day President Madison signed the declaration.

So the nation was at war even though the Massachusetts Federalists and their legislature urged its citizens not to cooperate in any way. They called it "Mr. Madison's War" and talked again of secession. Others referred to it as the "Second War of Independence." But whatever it was called, it had to be won and the prospects were not bright. Where would the money come from? How would the secretary of war manage? Everyone knew that Madison's secretary of war was not the most capable man. Few knew—not even Madison—if the newly appointed generals would be good. And President Madison himself, who had no experience in war, had a temperament more suited to reasoning than to fighting. But he was dogged, conscientious, and determined. When he went out now, he wore his little round hat with a huge cockade stuck in it, signifying that he was commander in chief.

What no one knew was that on May 11, while the *Hornet* was still at sea, England's prime minister, who had been the one most hostile to the United States, had been shot to death by a maniac. His cabinet resigned, and on June 16 the new English government repealed those orders which America had found so obnoxious—all but impressment. As it turned out, America began its war one day after war may no longer have been necessary, but no one would learn of this until much later. In any case, neither side could turn back now.

Nine

E ven before the fighting began, Americans were afraid that they were not getting the war off to a good start. In an emergency Americans had always declared a national day of prayer to make sure that God understood that they needed His special help. But when the people asked Madison to declare such a day, he said it was unconstitutional. The government couldn't tell people to pray. Finally at the insistence of Congress Madison did write a proclamation, but he worded it with care. He invited "societies so disposed to offer at one and the same time their common vows." Even though the result may have been the same, Madison was not interfering with the people's religious freedom.

But when the fighting actually started, it was obvious that the country did need help. No one could depend upon the generals. Two generals assigned to take key points in Canada turned tail and ran before even going into battle. At Detroit General William Hull with an army of 2500 surrendered to a tiny British force (less than 700) without firing a shot. Hull's own men were so mad, they threatened to shoot him. Newspapers called him a "booby" and the army court-martialed him with the recommendation that he be shot. Madison certainly didn't want him anywhere near a battle again, but why shoot him? He rejected the recommendation.

Then there was the case of General Smyth. In an attempt to take Fort Erie, he loaded his men into boats and sent an advance boat to the fort, demanding that the British surrender. As was to be expected, the British refused. So what did General Smyth do? He unloaded his boats and called off the battle. It was as if he thought it would be rude to argue with the enemy. And down went another general.

In the midst of these failures, Madison had to run for reelection. (Elbridge Gerry of Massachusetts was running as his vice president.) Naturally the Federalists blamed Madison for everything that went wrong. The war shouldn't have been started they said; it shouldn't be fought; it couldn't be won. Get rid of Madison. But the Federalists didn't have anyone to run against Madison so they backed an antiwar Republican, DeWitt Clinton. Everyone knew that if Madison lost, it would not only be a political defeat but also a military one, and far more serious than the downfall of two generals. Madison knew it too but he never said a word to promote his election. The people would have to decide for themselves, he said.

And they did. Soon after the beginning of the New Year (1813), the votes were finally all counted. Madison had 127 electoral votes, Clinton 89. Madison would stay in the President's Mansion, and in spite of threats of secession in New

England, the Union was still intact. The war would go on, but it did need good men to fight it. Madison, who always had trouble firing people, finally accepted the resignation of his secretary of war, but the new secretary, John Armstrong, was no better. Although he kept looking for good generals, Madison had little luck. The one man who would become the hero of this war had not yet been discovered.

As it turned out, Americans did much better at sea than on land, which was a surprise. Congress had consistently opposed spending much money to build up a navy. How could Americans hope to stop the British at sea? The British Navy was so huge, it had three warships for every American *gun.* Yet in the early days of the war three American ships defeated, captured, or destroyed three British vessels. Of course, American ships did not win every battle, but the reason they were so successful was that they fought differently. When the British fired their guns, they aimed at the masts of enemy ships to disable them. When the Americans fired, they aimed right at the waterline to sink them. The most spectacular victory of the war came in September 1813, when Captain Oliver Perry captured an entire British squadron on Lake Erie—two ships, two brigs, one schooner, one sloop. His message to the commanding general of the area has become famous in American history. "We have met the enemy and they are ours," he reported.

Madison received the news at Montpelier where he was recovering from such a serious "bilious" attack that the country feared he would die. John Adams, a firm supporter of Madison, said that Perry's victory "should be enough to revive Madison if he were in the last stages of consumption." And indeed when he returned to Washington, he was described as being "game as ever." But much had happened over the last year. Americans had retaken Detroit, had won a

Captain Perry's victory at Lake Erie

number of battles in Canada, and on April 27 they had seized the village of York (now Toronto). As it happened, York had burned to the ground soon after its capture and although Americans had not done this, Canadians and the British blamed them for it. In revenge they began burning American towns—Buffalo; Lewiston, Maine; and towns near Annapolis. British Admiral Cockburn (whose name rhymed with "go burn") threatened to march right into Washington and burn down the president's house. This sounded like enemy bluster even though a British frigate had been anchored at the mouth of the Potomac River since May 1813.

Still, there was also hope for peace. Russia had offered to negotiate between England and the United States, and although England had not as yet replied to the invitation, on May 9, 1813, Madison sent two delegates to Russia, ready to talk if England was willing. Payne Todd accompanied the delegates as a secretary, although he was not enthusiastic about going. Still handsome, still irresponsible, still a playboy, he was slated to go to Princeton, but Dolley and James thought a job and a year abroad would have a settling effect on "Precious Payne." Perhaps it might lead to a diplomatic career; at least it might make a man out of him. It did neither. After a few months in Russia, Payne slipped off to Paris to enjoy himself in his own way. Since he seldom wrote home, Dolley worried but at the same time tried to find excuses for him just as she always had.

It was not until the end of the year (1813) that England rejected Russia's offer. She wanted no intermediary; if she was going to negotiate, she would do it directly, and arrangements were made accordingly. Yet there seemed to be no change in England's attitude nor any great desire to promote peace—not even after England and France ended their war in March 1814. Surely with France out of the way, Americans thought, England would be more willing to come to terms with the United States. On the other hand, England was free now to unleash her full force against the United States, if that's what she wanted. Americans could only go on fighting.

The trouble was that not even Madison felt that Secretary of War John Armstrong was doing his best. Why, for instance, would anyone give two generals who were known to hate each other a joint command? Yet Armstrong did. He ordered these two generals to take Montreal, and when the campaign failed, he didn't tell Madison the exact truth about what happened. He often did not tell the exact truth. He often gave orders behind the president's back without his knowledge. Sometimes he didn't even let the president see his own mail; he just went ahead and answered, saying whatever he wanted. When Madison discovered what Armstrong had been doing, he told him straight out how much he disapproved of his actions. But he didn't fire him. Perhaps he had no one to replace him; perhaps he hoped the reprimand would change Armstrong. It didn't.

Indeed, Armstrong seemed to have no regard for the president's opinions. When Madison began predicting that the city of Washington was in danger, Armstrong paid no attention. As early as May 24, 1814, Madison was warning of an attack, but Armstrong did nothing. In June, when British Admiral Cockburn was already destroying property along Chesapeake Bay, Madison insisted that the city should be getting ready to defend itself. Secretary Armstrong scoffed at the idea. Finally, in desperation, Madison created a special military district around Washington. He gave the command to a General Winder with the recommendation that ten thousand men be called up to defend the area and that special units be set up to supply arms and ammunition. Secretary Armstrong did everything he could to thwart General Winder and, it seemed, the president himself. When the president ordered more men to be called up, Armstrong sent Winder his own order, which called for far fewer men. He sent his own order to Winder by *express* mail. He sent the president's order by regular mail, and it didn't reach Winder for twenty-two days. Even on August 18, when fifty-one British warships and transports were reported at the mouth of nearby Patuxent River, Armstrong refused to be alarmed. Why would the British bother with Washington, he asked? Baltimore was a much more likely target.

But the British headed for Washington. Armstrong, however, remained so casual, it was no wonder that blunders were made. Everything went wrong. Troops that should have been together were separated. The road that the enemy was using should have been blocked and wasn't. Both Winder and Madison himself had ordered that trees and every barricade available be laid across the road. Nothing was done. Later a British lieutenant said that if their way had been blocked, they would have surrendered. Winder, it turned out, was as inefficient as Armstrong was deceitful and stubborn. For four days James Madison rode about, trying to patch up the mistakes of one and uncover the deliberate mischief of the other. This small, gallant, sixty-four-year-old president, who couldn't have shouted to the troops if he'd wanted to, suddenly found himself not only the commander in chief in name but actually needing to take charge on the field. Even so, he probably didn't assert himself as strongly as he might have. He was not a Napoleon nor could he turn himself into one overnight. But he drove himself hard.

On August 22 when the citizens of Washington began abandoning the city to seek safety, Madison ordered the state papers—the letters of President Washington, the Declaration of Independence, and the Constitution—removed to Virginia. (Armstrong said there was no need to do this. Why panic?) Like her husband, Dolley was taking no chances. She sent her pet parrot to the house of the French ambassador, where she thought he'd be safe. James left to be with the army (such as it was), camped nine miles to the east.

Would Dolley be afraid to stay in the Mansion for a night or two until he was able to return? James asked.

Dolley was not the least bit afraid. She was just mad at the idea of British soldiers tramping into the President's Mansion, knocking around her lovely things, breaking them, stealing them, and perhaps setting fire to the house itself. James told her she should get ready for the worst. Pack up his personal papers and have them put in the carriage. But no personal belongings, he said. He stationed a hundred men as guard around the house and off he went.

For the next two days Dolley packed papers (four crates of them) and stationed herself at an upstairs window with her

Saving the Declaration of Independence

spy glasses to watch the hordes of people streaming out of the city. And because she needed someone to talk to, she wrote her sister Lucy—a breathless letter, a few words now, a few later as she jumped up to look out the window or to take care of another task.

"Our private property must be sacrificed," she wrote. "I am determined not to leave myself until I see Mr. Madison safe. . . . My friends and acquaintances are all gone."

But Dolley could not bear to part with all her private property. Perhaps at the last minute she could find a wagon to take an extra trunk or two. In any case, she packed some clothes (surely some turbans), the silverware, a few books, and her favorite clock. And she certainly wasn't going to leave those beautiful red velvet four-dollar-a-yard draperies for the British, so she yanked them down and packed them too.

On August 23 Madison questioned two British soldiers who had deserted. Yes, they said, the British were planning to attack Washington. Even now, Armstrong was not convinced. Maybe Annapolis, he said, not Washington, but Madison no longer had any patience with Secretary Armstrong. He wrote an urgent message to Dolley.

Dolley reported to her sister: "He desires that I should be ready at a moment's notice . . . to leave the city."

That evening Madison arrived back at the Mansion. He knew it would be a brief visit and as it turned out, it was both brief and interrupted. At dusk an officer arrived, explaining that the army needed arms and ammunition. Madison sent him to Armstrong, but hard as it is to believe, the incorrigible Armstrong told the officer it was too late to open the storehouse and closed the door in his face.

At nine o'clock General Winder came to report on the position of the troops—2500 camped near the Navy Yard at Washington, 2500 at Bladensburg, a village just east of Washington which the British would have to pass through in order to reach the capital. To have the army divided this way was not good news.

At midnight an urgent message was delivered to the president from the secretary of state, James Monroe. "The enemy are in full march on Washington," the message read. James and Dolley jumped out of bed, and with spy glasses in hand, they rushed up to the roof where they would have a better view. Nothing yet. At dawn Madison was off again—first to the Navy Yard and then to Bladensburg, where the battle would take place.

Often during the long day Dolley must have wandered about the Mansion, saying goodbye to one room after another. What she most hated leaving was that full length portrait of George Washington, but there it was—nailed to the wall. She did manage to secure a wagon and everything had been stowed in it. She had only to wait. She continued her letter to Lucy.

"Three o'clock—will you believe it, my sister? We have had a battle or skirmish near Bladensburg, and I am still here within the sound of cannon! Mr. Madison comes not; may God protect him!"

Hardly had she finished writing this when an army officer galloped up with a message from the president that Dolley should leave at once. Madison sent instruction as to where they would meet.

But now at the last minute Dolley knew that she could not leave President Washington's portrait behind. She ordered a servant to bring an ax and break the frame. Taking the portrait out of the frame, she had it put in the wagon. She knew she would be one of the last to leave the city, but still she took another minute to scribble down a final word to Lucy.

"It is done. . . . When I shall again write you or where I shall be tomorrow, I cannot tell."

She certainly could not tell. Dolley and James never did meet at the appointed place. Instead they fumbled through Virginia in the dark night, looking for each other, while

The portrait of Washington which Dolley saved

behind them the sky blazed with the reflection of a city on fire.

At nine o'clock in the evening the British had marched to the Capitol building, seated themselves in the House of Representatives, and in high good humor had voted unanimously to burn down the city. And they proceeded to do so, going from public building to public building, piling up woodwork and furniture and then setting it aflame. They reached the President's Mansion at about 10:30. Admiral Cockburn was in the lead, very much pleased with himself for carrying out his threat with such aplomb.

Seeing dinner laid out on the dining room table, he sat down, raised a glass of wine, and proposed a toast to James Madison's health. "Here! Here!" his men would have responded, just as delighted as he was to be where they were, doing what they were doing. Then they began ransacking the

The burning of Washington

house, picking up souvenirs as they went—rhinestone buckles, a medicine chest, a sword, a red velvet cushion, one of Madison's shirts, a package of his love letters, one of his hats (for the Admiral). When they left, each had a lighted torch in his hand. Once outside, they tossed them through the open windows, cheering as the flames caught, spread, and enveloped the mansion.

The next morning they might have continued their destruction except for a lucky accident. The weather, which so often decides the fate of a battle, let loose a giant hurricane on the city. Of course the British had storms in England, but these soldiers had seen nothing like this. This was a raging, terrifying affair that bent Mr. Jefferson's poplar trees on Pennsylvania Avenue to the ground, sent house roofs flying, knocked down walls, lifted up cannon, and killed thirty British soldiers. People had to lie down on the ground to keep the wind from picking them up and carrying them away. There was something eerie about it, as if the British had gone too far and were being punished. In any case, they decided they'd had enough and as soon as the storm let up a little, they returned to their ships. The damage, however, had been done. The battle of Bladensburg had been lost— needlessly, so the American officers claimed, and they informed Madison that they would not serve one hour longer under Secretary of War Armstrong. So Armstrong finally offered his resignation and Madison gave the double job of secretary of state and secretary of war to James Monroe.

As residents began returning to Washington, Dolley and James met at Dolley's sister Anna's house. Anna and her family, who were now living in Washington, invited the Madisons to stay. It was a gloomy place, Washington. Everyone was heartsick to see the blackened buildings, the skeleton of the President's Mansion, and the Capitol reduced to a pile of rubble, but no one felt worse than James Madison himself. One group of citizens decided that there was no point in fighting England any longer. They went to Madison and begged him to surrender.

Never, he said.

Others felt they should at least move the capital to Philadelphia.

No. Madison refused to give the British the satisfaction of thinking Americans could be chased out of their capital city.

Not everyone felt like giving up. Many all over the country were more determined than ever to beat the British. From all the surrounding states volunteers poured in to what appeared to be the next target—Baltimore. On September 11, Admiral Cochrane landed his fleet fourteen miles below Baltimore, but the Americans were ready. This time with a competent general they quickly drove back the British forces that had landed. Then, when the British ships turned their guns on Baltimore's Fort McHenry, the Americans stood firm through a twenty-four-hour bombardment. In the end the British retired in confusion.

A young American lawyer, Francis Scott Key, acting as a messenger for Madison, was held overnight on one of the British ships. From its deck he watched the entire battle and was so thrilled (especially at the sight of the American flag at "dawn's early light") that he wrote "The Star-Spangled Banner," and, of course, Americans have been celebrating the Fort McHenry victory ever since.

The news from Baltimore electrified the nation, particularly those in Washington whose pride had been hurt and whose confidence had been shaken. Yet the good news didn't stop there. Almost immediately the report arrived of a victory on Lake Champlain. One enemy frigate, one brig, and two sloops of war had been taken. How could the war go on

Octagon House

much longer? people asked each other. Yet it had been four months since the government had heard from the delegates negotiating for peace with England. What was going on?

The Madisons moved from Anna's house to what was called the Octagon House, loaned to them by the French ambassador. It was a queer place—not really eight-sided but six-sided with a bulge—and it was said to be haunted. Not superstitious, the Madisons paid no attention to this kind of talk, yet it was easy to see how such rumors started. In the dining room a sliding panel led to a secret passage and an underground tunnel. Moreover, some of the former occupants had met with strange accidents that were hard to explain. In one family, for instance, there had been two daughters; both fell in love with men of whom their father disapproved. Both girls at different times fell down the stairs of that house and were killed. Perhaps it was the ghosts of the girls that were supposed to do the haunting; perhaps their lovers. But it wasn't ghosts that bothered James and Dolley. The house was damp and chilly; the rooms were too small to accommodate many people, yet of course Dolley entertained. No matter what, Dolley would always entertain.

In October news finally arrived from the peace delegates. News about Payne too. All of it was bad. Payne was gambling and leading a wild life in Paris and although the delegates tried to persuade him to go home, he kept making up excuses. As for the peace negotiations, the report was that England was acting as if it still owned the colonies and could dictate its demands. Everything north of the Ohio River was to be declared Indian dominions—in other words, not open to American settlement. The Great Lakes were to be given to Canada; Maine was to be handed over to England. But what England most wanted was to possess New Orleans and take control of the West. Indeed, a large expedition had already sailed for New Orleans.

So the war stretched ahead. What John Adams had once said was still true. America had to prove to England and France and to itself that it was "not Nothing." Well, they would do it, Madison said.

Andrew Jackson

Ten

The country seemed to gather itself together to await the outcome of the battle that lay ahead at New Orleans. James Madison hoped against hope that the Commanding General, Andrew Jackson, would be equal to it. Jackson had won a decisive battle against the Creek Indians earlier in the year; he was reported to have strong personal reasons for hating the British; and he had a reputation of being a fiery fighter. "Old Hickory," his men called him because he was so tough, but Madison had counted on generals before who had disappointed him. He would simply have to wait and see.

It was hard to wait, but it was even harder to know that while he was waiting, New England Federalists were meeting in Hartford, Connecticut, to consider ways of opposing Madison and his war. Not a day passed without the Federalist press accusing Madison of being a tyrant, or of being incompetent, or of violating the Constitution. The Federalists insisted that there was no way that Americans could win this war. Of course these Federalist newspapers were read in England; of course such sentiments encouraged the British to prolong the fighting. A friend of Madison's contended that the Eastern states provided "the greatest, if not the sole, inducement with the enemy to persevere." But Madison, no matter what was said or how much he was slandered, would do nothing to try to keep those New England Federalists quiet. But naturally he was upset. Indeed, according to one observer, Madison looked "miserably shattered and woebegone. . . . His mind is full of the New England situation."

What would New England do? There were rumors of secession; rumors of New England making a separate peace with England; rumors of impeaching the president. "The bond of Union is broken," the delegates announced as they sought unconstitutional methods of changing the Constitution. In the end, however, the Hartford meeting decided to postpone any action until June. By that time, one member pointed out, the battle for New Orleans would be over and lost. Then what could Madison do but resign?

Meanwhile in a hotel in New Orleans General Andrew Jackson lay in bed, sick with dysentery. He had predicted that the enemy would avoid the swamps, the bayous, and the lakes that surrounded New Orleans and land instead at Mobile, Alabama, then march north and west to the city. He was wrong. The British commander, Major General Sir Edward Pakenham, landed a fleet of fifty ships and ten thousand troops at the entrance to a bay immediately east of New Orleans. General Pakenham not only carried a paper which would make him governor of Louisiana as soon as he conquered it but he had the promise of becoming an earl. Perhaps he was overanxious and did not take time to explore the nature of the terrain. Swamps, lakes, cedar forests—he had to drag his ten thousand men through all this before they reached a clearing near the Mississippi River on the morning of December 23, 1814. They were nine miles from the city.

When General Jackson heard where they were, he leaped out of his sickbed. "By the eternal," he cried, "we'll fight them tonight."

Jackson had only half as many troops as the British, but he assembled them quickly and marched down the river, reaching the British camp shortly after dark. Night battles, however, are seldom successful. After several hours of shooting blindly, Americans firing as often as not into other Americans, British into British, Jackson called off the attack.

There were several other attempts before the big battle of New Orleans took place on January 8, 1815. Jackson had picked his position carefully. Behind an abandoned canal,

Battle of New Orleans

Jackson's men had built a rampart high enough to reach a man's shoulders, thick enough to stop a cannonball. On the right was the Mississippi River, on the left was a swamp so the British would be forced to march over flat sugarcane fields toward that rampart where the Americans waited. After trying various maneuvers, the British, equipped with scaling ladders, decided to make simultaneous attacks on all sides of the rampart at the same time.

Right from the beginning, however, they were in trouble. Since they had to keep marching forward, they had no time to reload their guns. The Americans, on the other hand, fired all the time—not all together in systematic volleys as the British had been taught to do. When an American ran out of ammunition, he just ducked down behind the rampart, reloaded, then fired again—every man for himself in a continuous wall of fire. The battle actually lasted two hours, but most of the fighting was over in thirty minutes. Two thousand British soldiers were killed, wounded, or captured. Pakenham, shot in the neck, dropped from his horse and died almost immediately. As for the Americans, only thirteen men were lost—seven killed, six wounded.

And now they had to get the news to Washington. Unfortunately the weather was against them. There had been torrential rains, all the rivers were flooded, and it took almost a month for the news to arrive. Meanwhile the New England Federalists claimed that Madison was covering up a defeat at New Orleans. "Why hadn't Louisiana been properly defended?" they asked. "Go ask the wind," they said. Don't expect an answer from Madison.

On February 4 the news came. And Americans went wild. It was not only a victory; it was a landslide victory. And the British Navy? It was limping away from American waters. Every day the news became sweeter. Did you hear? Some of the very men who had set Washington on fire had been in the battle. Set off fireworks! Ring the bells! Light bonfires! Americans could not bear to stop celebrating. And why should they? This was the best news since Cornwallis had been defeated. And at last they had a war hero whom they could take to heart.

Ten days later, on February 14, when the people in Washington were just beginning to wind down from all their celebrating, a coach pulled by four horses careened down Pennsylvania Avenue and stopped short at the Madisons' Octagon House. A messenger with papers was admitted and dashed up the stairs to Madison's study, where he was meeting with his cabinet. A few moments later Madison came to the head of the staircase.

"Dolley," he shouted. "It's Peace!"

"Peace!" Dolley cried. She was so excited, she couldn't stop repeating the word. From room to room, to the servant's quarters, all over the house she ran. "Peace! Peace!" she sang. The servants rang the dinner bell and soon bells were ringing all over Washington. Apparently the messenger had already spread the news as his carriage sped through the city and everyone had simply burst into the streets, too happy to contain themselves inside. Dolley Madison threw open the doors to the Octagon House, ordered bottles to be opened, wine to be poured, and told the servants to light candles in every window.

This was the Treaty of Ghent signed by British and United States commissioners on December 24—fifteen days before the Battle of New Orleans had been fought. Had they known in time, the battle would not have been necessary, but perhaps in one sense it was lucky that they didn't know. The victory at New Orleans had given Americans a new confidence in themselves as an independent nation and the world had taken notice. Madison signed the peace treaty the same night as he received it, and the Senate ratified it the next day.

Now suddenly James Madison was a hero. Even his former critics were heaping praise on him and the Massachusetts legislature sent him an apology for the behavior of some of its citizens. Madison was little affected by all the superlatives flung in his direction. All he could think of was: the Union had survived. And he was weary. He had been in Washington eleven solid months, and he could hardly wait to get to Montpelier for a vacation.

He and Dolley left Washington at the end of March—earlier than usual and probably in time to catch the redbuds in bloom. Of course they didn't vacation alone; they never did, but there was one person whom Dolley longed to see at Montpelier above all others. Payne. Where was he? Peace had been signed; what possible excuse did he have to stay away longer? When some of the peace commissioners returned home, they brought with them trunks of Payne's clothes and artwork he had been collecting. As for Payne himself, all they could report was that he'd missed the boat in France and again in England.

Eventually he did appear that summer, tall and handsome as ever. In the more than two years that he had been away, however, he had picked up French manners and French taste and a habit of spending far more money than he had. His debts trailed him and would always trail him wherever he went. James paid them off as he could, but because they worried Dolley, he often kept secret the amount he was paying. As time went on, this secret ran to $40,000, and even so, Payne was twice put in debtor's prison for short periods. But right now James and Dolley still hoped that Payne would settle down and make a life for himself. But he did not want to go to Princeton, he said. He was too old and too experienced for that. He didn't know what he wanted. Perhaps he could just travel, but James would have none of that. No, Payne could serve as his secretary, and of course this pleased Dolley. Now she could stop worrying. "Precious Payne" would be with them, and when they returned to Washington, she would show Payne that Washington could be just as charming as Paris.

They returned in October—not to the Octagon House but to Seven Buildings, the former home of Vice President Gerry, who had died in office. The house was large, with thirty-one windows, and one had only to look out of the windows to see the president's old Mansion now under reconstruction two blocks away. The outside of the building was being repainted white and perhaps because this was such a welcome relief to the charred frame the British had left, people began calling it the White House. It would not be finished in time for Dolley to move in, but she was happy settling down in her new quarters close to the street and to passers-by. Whenever disbanded soldiers marched past, they always stopped in front of the house, raised their hats, and gave three cheers to Mrs. Madison. Huzza! Huzza! Huzza! they would cry and Dolley would come to the door, wave, and wish them well. Children would gather before the front window where they would watch Dolley feed and play with her pet parrot. When she had time, she would make a little show for the children.

There was a year and a half left to Madison's term of office and Dolley was determined to make the most of the time. Because she had so many parties and always illuminated those thirty-one windows, the house became known as "the house with a thousand candles." Perhaps her largest and most elaborate party was her New Year's Day open house and reception. For her 1816 New Year's reception, Dolley wore a new yellow satin dress embroidered with butterflies and a turban made of feathers. So many people crowded into this party that it was said that it took guests ten minutes to squeeze their way across the dining room. Then there was the February reception for the justices of the Supreme Court, the Peace Commissioners, and the diplomatic corps. For this, Dolley wore a rose-colored gown with what was described as a "mile-long" train of white velvet lined with lavender satin and edged with lace. Her turban was white velvet embroidered in gold and topped with ostrich feathers.

On Wednesday evenings she held her weekly receptions and so it went—one social affair after another. Everyone had hoped that General Jackson, the hero of New Orleans, would be present for the winter's activities, and although he and his wife did attend one ball in their honor, Jackson became ill and could not participate in other festivities. But in any case, wherever Dolley went, she stole the show. At one party people stood on benches to see Mrs. Madison in a dramatic black velvet dress trimmed in gold and wearing a tiara set with sapphires, which James had given her.

In March the following year (1817), when it came time for the newly elected president, James Monroe, to take office, the Madisons moved out of Seven Buildings into Dolley's sister Anna's house, to give Monroe ample room for his reception. They attended his inaugural ball but only briefly, for this was Monroe's night and they didn't want to distract attention from him. Still, because there were so many farewell parties for the Madisons, they could not leave Washington for another month. Everyone, it seemed, wanted to pay tribute to James Madison. Even John Randolph. He admitted that Madison was a "great man." As for Madison himself, he was just glad to announce that "the

American people had reached in safety and success their fortieth year as an independent nation."

He had done his job and it was with a light heart that he and Dolley boarded that new-fangled invention, the steamboat, to go down the Potomac River toward home. He was sixty-six years old and, a friend said, he talked and joked with everyone on board. He was like a "school Boy" setting out on a long vacation.

James

Dolley

Eleven

In retirement James and Dolley settled down to a kind of routine at Montpelier. After breakfast James might check the tin cup he kept at the gate to measure the rainfall. Then with whatever guests were present (and there were always guests) he would sit down facing the Blue Ridge Mountains and visit. Later in the morning, riding on his favorite horse, Liberty, he would make his daily inspection of the plantation, carrying with him his special cane, a crooked one that enabled him to open and shut gates without getting down from his horse. At two o'clock sharp he would visit his mother in her private quarters at Montpelier and sometime during the day he and Dolley would take a walk. They believed in regular exercise. If it was raining, they might race each other back and forth across the front porch.

Even when she reached sixty Dolley was a fast runner and proud of it.

Left to herself, Dolley read novels (she didn't like the gory ones) and she gardened. Wearing an enormous bonnet that she herself called "hideous," she would inspect the roses in the little walled English garden that James had built for her and if a particular flower took her fancy, she would name it for a person she loved. Occasionally she and James would ride to nearby relatives, but more often they would visit Jefferson at Monticello. Jefferson, feebler now in his old age, still rode his horse, Old Eagle, but he couldn't mount without help. No longer following public affairs as closely as James did, he was completely absorbed in the one project that was dearest to him—building the new University of Virginia in Charlottesville. James entered enthusiastically into Jefferson's plans and even after the university opened in 1825, he continued his strong support.

But perhaps the happiest time these three had together was in 1824 when General Lafayette came to America for a grand tour. Never in the history of America has a hero been given a more exuberant welcome. Wherever he went he was cheered, greeted with parades, banquets, firework displays. Although there were not many left who had actually known him, Lafayette had become a legend and an excuse for everyone to celebrate the Revolution once again. But to visit with old friends—that of course was the greatest treat. He went to Jefferson at Monticello, where James and Dolley joined them. Lafayette had changed. Just to look at him, James said, he would not have known Lafayette. He had grown very fat, but once he started talking he was his old ebullient self. And how wonderful it was to be together! They shared memories, laughed, and for that brief time they were all young again.

Throughout his retirement, however, James had private worries that plagued him. Money especially. He was running short of it. Like Washington and Jefferson before him, he had not been able to save anything from his president's salary ($25,000), and although he had counted on his crops to supplement his income, they had not done well. And of course it cost money to feed the constant stream of visitors (and their horses) who came to Montpelier. They were eating him out of "house and hay," Madison said.

And then there was Payne. No longer his stepfather's secretary, he had acquired 104 acres of land close to Montpelier where James and Dolley hoped he would finally settle down. Occasionally he did have ideas. Once he thought he'd raise silkworms and actually sent to France for people experienced in the business, but he never got around to sending for the silkworms. Once he thought he had marble on his property and planned to grow rich mining it. But he never did more than bring home rocks for his parents to admire. Always he was slipping off. Where, no one knew. All James could be certain of was that when he reappeared, he would be further in debt. And always he was.

But time kept moving ahead, occasionally lunging forward in ways that the Madisons found hard to accept. On July 4, 1826, on the fiftieth anniversary of the Declaration of Independence, both John Adams and Thomas Jefferson died. It was one of the most extraordinary coincidences in American history, yet this was exactly when Jefferson, who knew he had little time left, wanted to die. If he could only hold out until July 4! he said. Apparently this would give him the feeling of rounding out his circle of life, for he took pride in having written the Declaration of Independence. Just before he died, Jefferson handed his gold-topped walking cane to his doctor and asked him to deliver it personally to Madison.

A walking cane was perhaps a man's most intimate possession; Madison recognized the gift as the last acknowledgment of a long friendship. But how could he imagine a world without Jefferson at the top of his hill?

Time seemed to lunge forward again when in 1829 Andrew Jackson, the hero of New Orleans, became president, succeeding John Quincy Adams, who in turn had succeeded Monroe. America had grown and changed, no longer the small farming country in which Dolley and James had grown up. Now there were twenty-three states and the cities were crowded and industrialized. Up to this time men of property had run the government, but suddenly there was a cry from the common people and from those who lived in the West. They did not feel properly represented in Washington. But Andrew Jackson was a "man of the people;" he came from Tennessee and he would change all that. Still, some people did not like the idea of change at all. John Randolph, the eternal pessimist, announced, "The country is ruined past redemption."

James Madison, however, had always known that the country was bound to change and took a long view of the future. By 1929, he figured, America would probably have a population of one hundred and ninety-two million, but this did not worry him. He couldn't imagine what the country would be like, but of course it would have different kinds of people, many with new occupations and interests, expressing novel ideas. That was all right with Madison. Let the country expand, he said, only let it remember that the key to strength was Union. If *Union* had been the watchword of Madison's career, it was the very heartbeat of his old age.

Would he be a delegate to a Richmond convention to draft a new constitution for Virginia? Of course he would. The year was 1829 and Madison was seventy-eight years old, the last surviving member of the Federal Constitutional Convention of 1787. His voice was weaker than it had ever been, but if there was anything he could do to make the government work better, he wanted to do it. He wanted to try to extend voting privileges; he wanted to help the western part of the state feel that it had more share in the government. And if the constitution didn't turn out exactly as he wanted, he would still be glad he tried.

Would he become president of the American Colonization Society? He was eighty-four when this invitation came, but how could he refuse? The only solution to slavery still seemed to lie in resettling the slaves in colonies in Africa. Yet he knew this plan wasn't working. So far they had managed to ship off only two to three thousand slaves while every year the slave population increased by sixty thousand. Six of his own slaves, who could see the financial troubles of the Madisons, begged to be sold to a kind master rather than be sent to a country they had never seen. Reluctantly, Madison agreed. Yet he couldn't shake off his feeling of guilt and his fear. Slavery was dividing the land. Where would it lead?

Yet in 1832 a more direct threat had been hurled at the Union. The people of South Carolina did not like a new tariff that others said favored the North and imposed a hardship on them. And if a state did not like a law, according to John C. Calhoun of South Carolina, a state need not obey it. He called this the doctrine of nullification and he went further. If the federal government tried to force a state to obey a law it didn't like, the state had every right to secede from the Union. He said there was a precedent for this view. Madison and Jefferson had, themselves, implied just such an idea in the Virginia and Kentucky Resolves which they had written to oppose John Adams's Alien and Sedition Acts.

No! Not true! Madison picked up his pen and replied in no uncertain terms. He and Jefferson had simply been *protesting,* which was a lawful procedure. State power could never simply throw off federal law as if it were just so much trash. Calhoun was "putting powder under the Constitution," and as long as James Madison had breath in his body, he would oppose him. He was relieved to learn that Andrew Jackson felt as strongly as he did. "To say that any state may at pleasure secede from the Union," Jackson stated, "is to say that the United States is not a nation." What was more, Jackson privately threatened that "if one drop of blood be shed . . . in defiance of the laws of the United States, I will hang the first man of them I can get my hands on to the first tree I can find." Eventually the danger of nullification subsided as the tariff was reduced, but Madison remained uneasy about the future. South Carolina, by putting forward the idea of nullification, had encouraged a spirit of disunion.

It seemed more important than ever to Madison that he get his notes on the Constitutional Convention in proper shape so that they could be printed after his death. He felt sure that the government would buy his notes and publish them, for certainly future generations should know what took place in Philadelphia. In order to preserve the Constitution, they would need to understand the thinking of the Framers and what they had sacrificed to bring about the compromises that not only made their Union possible but were meant to make it endure.

Over the last years, as he was finishing the work, he was often bedridden with arthritis. His handwriting, he told a friend, became smaller as he grew older and his steps shorter. There were months when he couldn't write at all and then Dolley sat at his bedside, taking notes for hours at a time. It was a tedious business, she said. Sometimes when she was working alone, she kept a music box playing at her side, but the work was getting done.

By the middle of June in 1836 it was clear that James Madison could not survive much longer. Perhaps, his friends said, he could hold out until July Fourth. Five years before, James Monroe became the third president to die on July Fourth. It seemed to have become almost a tradition for great Americans to die on that day. Madison was asked if he would like the doctor to try to keep him alive until that date, but Madison said No. He was eighty-five years old now and at peace with himself. He had a last message, however, that he wanted to leave the country.

"The advice nearest my heart and deepest in my conviction," he said, "is that the Union of States be cherished and perpetuated."

On the morning of June 27, when his niece brought his breakfast to him, he said he didn't want it.

"What is the matter, Uncle James?" she asked.

"Nothing more than a change of mind, my dear," he replied. His head dropped on his pillow and he stopped breathing.

What did he mean? Had he thought that perhaps he might hold out until July Fourth without the doctor's help? Was he referring to the change that death brings? Or was he simply saying he had changed his mind about breakfast? No one will know.

He was buried in the family plot a half a mile south of the house. His tombstone was in the shape of an obelisk, which was the fashion of the day, but the inscription simply read MADISON. No first name was needed. For the country, as well as Dolley, there was only one Madison.

Dolley lived for thirteen more years, but because her estate was so mismanaged by Payne, she had to sell Montpelier and move to Washington. She reentered Washington society like a returning queen and was welcomed as such. She held open house on New Year's Day and on July Fourth just as she always had, and when she died at the age of eighty-one, she was buried in Washington. Her many friends, however, recognized that this was not the right resting place for Dolley. They raised money by subscription, and about ten years later she was moved to the little family plot in Montpelier. She took her place beside Madison, which is where she belonged.

Notes

Page 10. Most young men entered college earlier in their teens. John Adams entered Harvard when he was fifteen.

Page 14. The Continental Congress, which met first in 1774, was not a legislative body but a gathering of delegates from the colonies with authority derived simply from public opinion. Nevertheless, it created the Continental Army and directed the war. In November 1777, it agreed upon a framework for government under the Articles of Confederation, although these Articles were not ratified until 1781.

Page 42. For purposes of representation in the House, the population of each state, as stated in the final wording of the Constitution, "shall be determined by adding to the whole Number of free persons, including those bound to Service for a Term of Years, and excluding Indians not taxed, three-fifths of all other Persons." In other words, a slave counted as three-fifths of a person.

Page 50. Dorothea was Patrick Henry's second wife. His first wife, Sarah, had died some years before.

Page 57. The Bill of Rights consists of ten amendments proposed by James Madison. These amendments spell out an individual's inalienable rights and were modeled after the Virginia Declaration of Rights.

Page 70. Although many people during her life and later spelled her name "Dolly" and some thought it was a nickname for Dorothea, Dolley's name was officially spelled with an "e" both on her birth certificate and again on her tombstone.

Page 78. The Twelfth Amendment, passed in 1804, changed this procedure for electing the vice president. It was established then that the electors would cast separate ballots for president and vice president.

Page 81. Kentucky had become a state in 1792.

Page 82. Patrick Henry died in June 1799, before the legislature met.

Page 93. Virginia was filled with Randolphs, all interrelated. John Randolph was known as John Randolph of Roanoke and though related to Edmund, he was not in his immediate family.

Page 100. "Strike her colors" means that the ship lowered its flag completely as a sign of surrender.

Page 117. DeWitt Clinton was a nephew of George Clinton.

Page 120. Napoleon, weakened after a disastrous expedition to Russia, was defeated in Paris on March 31, 1814, by England and its allies. Napoleon abdicated, and although he tried to make a brief comeback the following year, he was crushed at the Battle of Waterloo (June 1815).

Page 133. As a fourteen-year-old prisoner of the British in the Revolutionary War, Andrew Jackson had refused to polish a British officer's boots. The British officer slashed him with his sword and he bore the scar for the rest of his life.

Page 139. There are various stories about when the President's Mansion was first called the White House. Some say it began from a joke made when Andrew Jackson was in office, but no one remembers the joke. In any case, Congress officially designated it the White House in 1902, although the name was commonly used even while the Madisons were alive.

Page 141. They went by boat as far as Aquia Creek, where they were met by a carriage.

Page 147. Dolley had a wonderful three months in Richmond. A journalist reported that at sixty-one, Dolley Madison was "a stout, tall, straight woman, muscular but not fat, and as active on her feet as a girl." But the jet black curls that hung down from her turbans were no longer her own. They were store-bought.

Page 149. Madison had to admit that in Jefferson's original draft, he had used the word "nullify," but Jefferson hadn't really meant it, he said. Jefferson was a man of broad vision who often simply rounded off his phrases.

Page 149. Congress did eventually buy Madison's notes for $30,000, but after Dolley had paid the other beneficiaries to the will, there was only $9,000 left for herself. Madison had expected the notes to bring $50,000.

Page 151. Congress bought James's private papers and in order to protect this money from Payne, they paid Dolley an annual sum on which she was able to live.

Bibliography

Adams, John, and Thomas Jefferson. *The Adams-Jefferson Letters.*
Edited by Lester J. Cappon. 2 vols. Chapel Hill, North Carolina:
University of North Carolina Press, 1959,

Anthony, Katherine. *Dolley Madison. Her Life and Times.* Garden
City, New York: Doubleday & Company, 1949.

Ayers, James. *We Hold These Truths: From the Magna Carta to the
Bill of Rights.* Reprint. New York: Henry Holt & Company,
1985.

Banner, James J., Jr. *To the Hartford Convention.* New York: Alfred
A. Knopf, 1970.

Bowen, Catherine Drinker. *Miracle at Philadelphia: The Story of the
Constitutional Convention, May to September, 1787.* Boston: At-
lantic-Little, Brown, 1966.

Brant, Irving. *James Madison.* 6 vols. Indianapolis, Indiana: Bobbs-
Merrill, 1941–1961.

———. *The Fourth President. A Life of James Madison.*
Indianapolis, Indiana: Bobbs-Merrill, 1970.

Clark, Allen. *The Life and Letters of Dolley Madison.* Washington,
D. C.: W. F. Roberts Company, 1914.

Daniels, Jonathan. *The Randolphs of Virginia.* Garden City, New
York: Doubleday & Company, 1972.

Dauer, Manning J. *The Adams Federalists.* Baltimore: Johns Hopkins
University Press, 1953.

Dawidoff, Robert. *The Education of John Randolph.* New York: W.
W. Norton, 1979.

Desmond, Alice Curtis. *Glamorous Dolly Madison.* New York: Dodd,
Mead & Company, 1946.

Eidelberg, Paul. *The Philosophy of the American Constitution: A Rein-
terpretation of the Intention of the Founding Fathers.* Lanham,
Maryland: University Press of America, 1986.

Farrand, Max. *Records of the Constitutional Convention.* 4 vols. Reprint. New Haven, Connecticut: Yale University Press, 1966.

———. *The Framing of the Constitution of the United States.* New
Haven, Connecticut: Yale University Press, 1913.

Gay, Peter. *The Enlightenment: An Interpretation; The Rise of Mod-
ern Paganism.* New York: Random House/Vintage Books, 1966.

Hunt-Jones, Conover. *Dolley and the Great Little Madison.* Washington, D. C.: American Institute of Architects Foundation, 1977.

Jensen, Merrill. *The Founding of a Nation.* New York: Oxford University Press, 1968.

Kammen, Michael. *A Machine That Would Go of Itself: The Constitution in American Culture.* New York: Alfred A. Knopf, 1986.

——, editor. *The Origins of the American Constitution: A Documentary History.* New York: Viking-Penguin, 1986.

Ketcham, Ralph. *James Madison. A Biography.* New York: Macmillan Publishing Company, 1971.

Koch, Adrienne. *Power, Morals, and the Founding Fathers.* Ithaca, New York: Cornell University Press, 1961.

Madison, James. *Letters and Other Writings.* 4 vols. Philadelphia: J. B. Lippincott Company, 1865.

Malone, Dumas. *Jefferson and His Times.* 5 vols. Boston: Little, Brown & Company, 1948–1975.

Miller, John C. *Crisis in Freedom: The Alien and Sedition Acts.* Boston: Little, Brown & Company, 1952.

——. *The Federalist Era, 1789–1801.* New York: Harper & Row, 1960.

Moore, Virginia. *The Madisons: A Biography.* New York: McGraw-Hill, 1979.

Morris, Richard B. *The Forging of a Union, 1781–1789.* New York: Harper & Row, 1987.

——. *Witnesses at the Creation: Hamilton, Madison, Jay, and the Constitution.* Reprint. New York: Henry Holt & Company, 1985.

Nevins, Allan. *The American States During and After the Revolution, 1775–1789.* New York: Macmillan Publishing Company, 1924.

Peterson, Merrill. *James Madison: A Biography in His Own Words.* New York: Newsweek Books, 1974.

Rutland, Robert A. *James Madison: The Founding Father.* New York: Macmillan Publishing Company, 1987.

Wills, Garry. *Explaining America: The Federalist.* New York: Penguin, 1981.

Wood, Gordon S. *The Creation of the American Republic, 1776–1787.* Chapel Hill, North Carolina: University of North Carolina Press, 1969.

Index

Illustration credits

AMERICAN ARCHITECTURAL FOUNDATION/THE OCTAGON MUSEUM, Washington, D.C.: p. 130, photo by John Tennant

ATWATER KENT MUSEUM, Philadelphia, PA: p. 75

THE BETTMANN ARCHIVE: p. 38; p. 40, engraving by J.A.J. Wilcox, SC; p. 45; p. 49, painting by Clyde O. Deland, 1915; p. 98; p. 111; p. 119; p. 123, drawing by B. West Clinedinst; p. 135, Kurz and Allison, lithographers

BOWDOIN COLLEGE MUSEUM OF ART: p. 67, portrait by Gilbert Stuart, 1805–1807

ANNE S.K. BROWN MILITARY COLLECTION, BROWN UNIVERSITY LIBRARY: p. 127

GILCREASE MUSEUM, Tulsa, Oklahoma: p. 2, painting by Charles Willson Peale

THE GREENSBORO HISTORICAL MUSEUM, Greensboro, NC: p. 107

THE HISTORICAL SOCIETY OF PENNSYLVANIA: stamping, front cover, from a silhouette of Madison by Joseph Sansom, 1781; p. 15, illustration by William Birch & Son

LIBRARY OF CONGRESS: p. 9; p. 11, miniature by Charles Willson Peale; p. 27, miniature by Charles Willson Peale; p. 41

JAMES MADISON MUSEUM: p. 79; p. 151

MASSACHUSETTS HISTORICAL SOCIETY p. 34, portrait by Joseph Boze, 1790

NATIONAL TRUST, Montpelier: p. 105, bust by William Coffee

NEW YORK PUBLIC LIBRARY: p. 18, portrait etched by Albert Rosenthal, 1888; p. 43, portrait by William Sartain; p. 55, engraving (ca 1790) by Amos Doolittle, after a drawing by Peter Lacour; p. 84, engraving by John James Barralet; p. 87, by C.W. Jansen; p. 94; p. 102; p. 132, engraving by A.B. Durand, after a portrait by John Vanderlyn

PENNSYLVANIA ACADEMY OF THE FINE ARTS: p. 68, portrait by Gilbert Stuart, 1804

PRINCETON UNIVERSITY LIBRARY: p. 12, Doolittle engraving of Nassau Hall

SMITHSONIAN INSTITUTION: p. 89

THOMAS JEFFERSON PAPERS, UNIVERSITY OF VIRGINIA LIBRARY: p. 29

VIRGINIA HISTORICAL SOCIETY: pp. 142, 143, portraits by Joseph Wood, 1817

WHITE HOUSE HISTORICAL ASSOCIATION: p. 22; p. 126, portrait by Gilbert Stuart

MAPS on pp. 6, 32 and 92 by Anita Karl and James Kemp